T0334088

Cambridge Elements ≡

Elements in the Philosophy of Ludwig Wittgenstein
edited by
David G. Stern
University of Iowa

WITTGENSTEIN
ON RELIGIOUS BELIEF

Genia Schönbaumsfeld
University of Southampton

CAMBRIDGE
UNIVERSITY PRESS

Shaftesbury Road, Cambridge CB2 8EA, United Kingdom

One Liberty Plaza, 20th Floor, New York, NY 10006, USA

477 Williamstown Road, Port Melbourne, VIC 3207, Australia

314–321, 3rd Floor, Plot 3, Splendor Forum, Jasola District Centre, New Delhi – 110025, India

103 Penang Road, #05–06/07, Visioncrest Commercial, Singapore 238467

Cambridge University Press is part of Cambridge University Press & Assessment, a department of the University of Cambridge.

We share the University's mission to contribute to society through the pursuit of education, learning and research at the highest international levels of excellence.

www.cambridge.org
Information on this title: www.cambridge.org/9781009276054

DOI: 10.1017/9781009276061

First published 2023

A catalogue record for this publication is available from the British Library.

ISBN 978-1-009-27605-4 Paperback
ISSN 2632-7112 (online)
ISSN 2632-7104 (print)

Wittgenstein on Religious Belief

Elements in the Philosophy of Ludwig Wittgenstein

DOI: 10.1017/9781009276061
First published online: January 2023

Genia Schönbaumsfeld
University of Southampton

Author for correspondence: Genia Schönbaumsfeld, gmes@soton.ac.uk

Abstract: Wittgenstein published next to nothing on the philosophy of religion and yet his conception of religious belief has been both enormously influential and hotly contested. In the contemporary literature, Wittgenstein has variously been labelled a fideist, a non-cognitivist and a relativist of sorts. This Element shows that all of these readings are misguided and seriously at odds, not just with what Wittgenstein says about religious belief, but with his entire later philosophy. This Element also argues that Wittgenstein presents us with an important 'third way' of understanding religious belief – one that does not fall into the trap of either assimilating religious beliefs to ordinary empirical beliefs or seeking to reduce them to the expression of certain attitudes.

Keywords: Wittgenstein, religion, Christianity, science, Kierkegaard, faith, God

ISBNs: 9781009276054 (PB), 9781009276061 (OC)
ISSNs: 2632-7112 (online), 2632-7104 (print)

Contents

1 Introduction

1.1 Overview

Wittgenstein's conception of religious belief is quite radical: 'If Christianity is the truth, then all the philosophy written about it is false' (*Culture and Value* (CV) 89/83[1]). This is not a pronouncement that has served to endear Wittgenstein to many philosophers of religion or militant atheists seeking to debunk religious belief. For the former think that Wittgenstein has eviscerated religious belief of serious content, while the latter believe that what Wittgenstein is offering is a recherché form of apologetics. I doubt that anything I say in this Element will change this. Nonetheless, I will try to show that both characterizations are wide of the mark – Wittgenstein's conception of religious belief, just as his writing more generally, intends to challenge the often philosophically complacent assumptions that drive these verdicts.[2]

A work of this length inevitably has to be highly selective and concentrate on what the author takes to be the most important aspects of the overall narrative. Consequently, the debate sometimes takes place with a small group of suspects (a wider overview of the literature is provided in the footnotes). But the respective interlocutors have been chosen because they are representatives of major lines of argument that continue to dominate contemporary discussion.

I also make no apology for concentrating primarily on Christian religious belief. This is the religion that Wittgenstein was brought up in and that he grappled with during his entire life. Moreover, many of Wittgenstein's insights generalize and can fruitfully be applied to Islam and Judaism, just as much as to Christianity.[3]

This Element is composed of six sections, each with their own subsections. It presupposes no prior knowledge of Wittgenstein's work and aims to be accessible. Its desire is solely for an open-minded reader, who, 'in the darkness of this time',[4] seeks a new way of making sense of religious belief.

1.2 Wittgenstein's Philosophical Method

In order to understand Wittgenstein's conception of religious belief, we must first understand Wittgenstein's philosophical method. For there is an intimate

---

[1] The first page reference is to the newer edition of *Culture and Value*, the second one to the older version.

[2] For my own first attempt in this direction, see Schönbaumsfeld (2007).

[3] In this respect, see Sievers and Suleiman (in press). Also see Gorazd Andrejc and Daniel Weiss (2019).

[4] Preface to *Philosophical Investigations*.

connection between central themes in Wittgenstein's later work, *Philosophical Investigations* (PI), and Wittgenstein's thoughts on religious belief that appear in various different posthumously published collections, not all of which were directly penned by Wittgenstein himself (such as, for example, the *Lectures and Conversations on Religious Belief* and Wittgenstein's *Cambridge Lectures* (CL) (1930–3)). Since PI was always intended by Wittgenstein for publication and this work constitutes Wittgenstein's most considered views, I adopt the exegetical principle that PI be given priority when it comes to ascertaining what implications Wittgenstein's oeuvre has for a conception of religion.[5] Once these pieces of the puzzle are in place, it will be much easier to make sense of all the other available material that concerns religious matters more directly. This way of proceeding also has the advantage that remarks that are derived from lecture notes (such as the *Lectures and Conversations on Aesthetics, Psychology and Religious Belief* (LC) and CL 1930–3) can be assessed against Wittgenstein's overall philosophical concerns.

Wittgenstein not only invented a new philosophical method – which he once described as similar to the shift from alchemy to chemistry[6] – he also used it in an iconoclastic manner, in order to *dissolve*, rather than solve, the great philosophical problems of the past. Philosophy is, therefore, not a body of knowledge for Wittgenstein, but an *activity* of grammatical (conceptual) clarification or elucidation[7]: 'Philosophy is a struggle against the bewitchment of our understanding by the resources of our language' [*die Mittel unserer Sprache*] (PI §109). Wittgenstein's method is devised to liberate us from the spell that language casts by freeing us from the conceptual confusions and illusions that hold us in thrall and which we take for genuine problems requiring a theoretical solution. But if Wittgenstein is right that philosophical problems turn out to be illusory pseudo-problems that only appear to make sense for as long as one remains within their grip, then these cannot be addressed in a standard theoretical manner. For this presupposes that we are confronted by a genuine claim that one might refute, rather than by a confusion that can only be undermined or dissolved.

---

[5] Religious reflections also play an important part in Wittgenstein's early writings, such as the *Notebooks* (1984) and the *Tractatus Logico-Philosophicus* (TLP), but these works are hamstrung by Wittgenstein's early conception of language, which ultimately confined religious questions to the realm of the ineffable. For this reason, my main focus will be the later work, as its implications for a conception of religious belief are much more profound. I will, however, be making reference to the early work where pertinent and appropriate. For more in-depth discussion of early Wittgenstein's significance for religion, see Schönbaumsfeld (2007, 2013, 2018a).

[6] Quoted in Monk (1991: 298).

[7] This was a view that Wittgenstein already held in the *Tractatus Logico-Philosophicus* (TLP) and that he never changed his mind on, despite his later conception of philosophy being in many respects very different from his earlier one.

That such a conception of philosophy could be perceived as destructive – both in Wittgenstein's time as well as in our own – Wittgenstein himself seems well aware:

> Where does this investigation get its importance from, given that it seems only to destroy everything interesting: that is, all that is great and important? (As it were, all the buildings, leaving behind only bits of stone and rubble.) But what we are destroying are only houses of cards [*Luftgebäude*], and we are clearing up the ground of language on which they stood. (PI §118)

But to get someone to see that it is only *Luftgebäude* ('castles in the air' would be a closer rendition of the notion than 'houses of cards') that are being destroyed – not something genuinely great and important – is extraordinarily difficult. For *Luftgebäude* look, when viewed from a certain perspective, very much like imposing buildings. Consequently, it is easy to become attached to these appearances and to be resistant to anyone wishing to expose them for what they are: bits of stone and rubble that a grammatical conjuring trick (PI §308) has turned into an estate of palatial proportions.

In order to achieve clarity in philosophy, it is consequently imperative that one learn to resist the lure of what one wants to see, in favour of giving the facts – the way things actually are – their due. This means not allowing oneself to be taken in by the 'surface grammar' of our words (how they appear to function linguistically in a sentence):

> In the use of words, one might distinguish 'surface grammar' from 'depth grammar'. What immediately impresses itself upon us about the use of a word is the way it is used in the sentence structure, the part of its use – one might say – that can be taken in by the ear. – And now compare the depth grammar, say of the verb 'to mean', with what its surface grammar would lead us to presume. No wonder one finds it difficult to know one's way about. (PI §664)

The surface grammar of the verb 'to mean', its similarity to 'action' verbs like 'to wash' or 'to write', suggests that it is the name of a mental, as opposed to a physical, process going on in the hidden medium of 'the mind', whereas Wittgenstein's conceptual investigation shows that its depth grammar (how the word really functions) is actually quite different. Rather than referring to a hidden process, 'to mean' is much more similar to the concept of having an ability: a competent language-user can mean 'X' rather than 'Y', not because something special goes on in their mind (or brain), but because they are generally able to apply the words 'X' and 'Y' with facility. Whether a speaker meant 'X' or 'Y' can, therefore, be determined, not by looking into the speaker's mind, but by ascertaining whether the speaker has mastered a particular technique, what the speaker goes on to say and do, what consequences the speaker would be prepared (or not prepared) to draw, etc.

So, when Wittgenstein says, at PI §122, that our grammar is deficient in surveyability, what he means is that the 'depth grammar' is still unclear to us. All we see is the surface grammar, the mere syntactical structure of the word or sentence – 'the use that can be taken in by the ear' – not the actual use, what early Wittgenstein would have called the 'logical syntax' of the sign: the rules for the correct use of the word, which can be hidden underneath the word's apparent use (the 'surface grammar') in the way that the real form of a body may be obscured by a person's clothes (TLP 4.002).

Attending to the 'depth grammar', however, requires a willingness to look beyond the surface; to refuse to be taken in by superficial linguistic appearances that may lead one astray. This is difficult, as the surface appearance may be attractive and tempt us to want to continue to view the problem in the accustomed manner. For this reason, Wittgenstein thinks that the struggle for clarity requires both an intellectual effort and an engagement of the will. We need the intellectual acumen to see through the deceptive appearances, but also require the willpower to resist bewitchment by grammar: 'A *picture* held us captive. And we couldn't get outside it, for it lay in our language, and language only seemed to repeat it to us inexorably' (PI §115).

Because our language is full of substantives, for example, and we naively assume that the meaning of a word is the object it refers to – Wittgenstein calls this Augustine's picture of language – if we are unable actually to find such an object in the world, we take it that there must be a 'supernatural' object or spirit that the word can refer to instead: 'Where our language suggests a body and there is none: there, we should like to say, is a *spirit* [*Geist*]' (PI §36). Arguably, this temptation motivated Plato's theory of the Forms – the 'Form of the Good' or of 'Beauty' can never be found in the myriad different objects we actually apply the words 'good' or 'beautiful' to, but only in a metaphysical realm of 'Forms' populated by the abstract objects that are the alleged referents of these unadulterated essences. As Wittgenstein says in the *Remarks on Frazer's Golden Bough* (RFGB) §25: 'Here the image used in thinking of reality is that beauty, death, etcetera are the pure (concentrated) substances, and that they are present in a beautiful object as an admixture.' Similarly, many mathematicians (including philosophers of mathematics) think that since number words cannot refer to empirical objects in the world, they must refer instead to abstract objects. Relatedly, philosophers of religion, theologians and ordinary religious people often believe that the word 'God' is the name of a supernatural object or entity.

What we are primarily taken in by, in such cases, is the fact that words like 'beauty', 'one' and 'God', appear to operate in exactly the same way as more ordinary words whose referents we can straightforwardly point to, such as 'cat', 'table' and 'chair'. From this we draw the conclusion that in the former case, too, there must be objects these words stand for, it's just that they happen not to be empirically locatable.

Augustine's picture of language, in other words, seems natural and intuitive, as it reduces the diversity of the actual function of words to an easily graspable common denominator: 'the words in language name objects – sentences are combinations of such names' (PI §1). Wittgenstein himself was tempted by something like such a view in his early work, the *Tractatus*. Later, however, Wittgenstein realizes that language is not as uniform as Augustine's picture would have us believe. There are many different kinds of word and they do not all function as names: 'Someone who describes the learning of language in this way [by ostensive definition] is, I believe, thinking primarily of nouns like "table", "chair", "bread", and of people's names, and only secondarily of the names of certain actions and properties; and of the remaining kinds of word as something that will take care of itself' (PI §1). Naturally, the remaining kinds of word do *not* take care of themselves, which is why philosophers tend to invent abstract entities in order to explain how these words can function like names after all.

Rather than trying to press the diversity of the functions of words into a uniform mould that distorts them, Wittgenstein suggests that we would do better to abandon our preconceived idea that the essence of language consists in naming, for this would enable us to see that the role that a word plays in language is complex and cannot be reduced to an attitude of 'one size fits all'. 'Think just of exclamations', Wittgenstein says, 'with their completely different functions. Water! Away! Ow! Help! Splendid![8] No! Are you still inclined to call these words "names of objects"?'(PI §27).

Whether a word functions as the name of an object – and Wittgenstein does not deny that some words are names[9] – is not something that can be settled independently of attending to the context in which the word is used. It is the overall role the word plays in the language-game or linguistic practice that tells us what kind of word it is and what it does. This is why Wittgenstein says: 'For a *large* class of cases of the employment of the word "meaning" – though not for *all* – this word can be explained in this way: the meaning of a word is its use in the language' (PI §43). Just as the significance of the different chess pieces can be explained by describing the moves these pieces can make in the game of chess, so the significance of a word can be explained by looking at how the word is employed in a particular language-game. This is not to advance a new theory

---

[8] In PI these words occur as separate paragraphs. For ease of reading, I have removed these spaces.
[9] Neither does he deny that (some) words refer to objects. What he does deny is that the meaning is something independent of the word that can be reified (either an empirical or an abstract object).

of meaning – hence the warning that Wittgenstein's suggestion is not meant to apply across the board – but to provide us with the tools to free ourselves from enslavement to the Augustinian picture that made us believe that there is only one way for language to operate.

1.3 Theology and Grammar

Although religious questions were of the first importance to Wittgenstein – something testified to by his various conversations with friends,[10] his lectures[11] as well as his own reflections scattered throughout, for example, the early *Notebooks*, and, in particular, the volume that has come to be known as *Culture and Value* – in PI itself, there is only one direct allusion to a religious theme:

> *Essence* is expressed in grammar (PI §371).

> Grammar tells what kind of object anything is. (Theology as grammar.)
> (PI §373)

Wittgenstein believes that one of the main confusions that arise in philosophy (and elsewhere) is to mistake a grammatical (logical) feature of a concept for an empirical description and to end up predicating of the thing what lies in the mode of representation (PI §104). The comparison with theology and the concept of 'God' serves to make this perspicuous (which is perhaps why theology is the first thing that occurs to Wittgenstein in this regard). A passage from the recently published lectures from the early 1930s throws more light on what Wittgenstein might have in mind here:

> Now (a) suppose 'god' means something like a human being; then 'he has 2 arms' & 'he has 4 arms' are not grammatical propositions but (b) suppose someone says: You can't talk of god having arms, this is grammatical.
> (CL 321)

If we think the word 'God' is the name of something very akin to a human being, then saying that this god has two or four arms would not be different from offering a straightforward empirical description of something, for example, 'this animal has two legs' or 'this animal has four legs'. Here we are describing something contingent that could be otherwise, had the world been different in some way. But if we say something like 'It makes no sense to speak of God having arms', then we are making a grammatical remark that shows that it is part

---

[10] See Wittgenstein's conversations with Maurice Drury (in Rhees (1984)), Norman Malcolm (1993, 2001) and Rush Rhees (2001), for instance.

[11] See, for example, the aforementioned CL, LC and RFGB.

of the concept of God that we can't attribute certain physical features to him – it's not that God is an entity who just happens not to have these characteristics.

The essential features of our concepts are specified by the grammar of the concept. To give a non-theological example, to say that 'one is a number' is not to attribute some predicate (that of numberhood) to an abstract object, but to tell us how the word 'one' functions in our language – namely, as a number-word. To say that 'red is a colour' is similarly to say something about the grammar of 'red', not to give a description of an esoteric object. To think otherwise is precisely to predicate of the thing what lies in the mode of representation: to believe one is tracing the thing's nature when in fact you are giving a rule for the correct use of a word (i.e. something grammatical).

Many philosophical and theological problems arise if one doesn't heed this distinction. If, for instance, one believes that the word 'God' functions like the name of a 'gaseous vertebrate',[12] then it would make sense to ask where such an entity could be found, whether it had certain (invisible) physical features, if it ever got bored, etc. Wittgenstein thinks that such questions are nonsensical. As he says in a late conversation with Rhees: 'Our statements about God have a different grammar from our statements about human beings. And if you try to talk about God as you would talk about a human being, you are likely to come to talk nonsense, to ask nonsensical questions and so on' (Rhees, 2001: 413).

Why does Wittgenstein think that one would come to speak nonsense if one tried to talk about God as one would about a human being? Primarily, because this betrays a category mistake: God is not a 'gaseous vertebrate' with invisible stomach and toenails. To think otherwise is to turn the concept of God into that of an idol (into an in principle perceivable entity, such as a Golden Calf, for example, or a god who lives on Mount Olympus), and this, in the Christian (and, perhaps, other monotheistic religious traditions), would also be blasphemous.

Now one might think that, apart from some militant atheists who believe that people engage in religious practices out of sheer stupidity – a notion that Wittgenstein particularly criticizes in the case of English anthropologist, Frazer, who interpreted the magical rituals of primitive tribes as forms of false science[13] – there are not many theologians or religious believers who would be happy to ascribe such a crude grammar to the word 'God'. But such an appearance would be deceptive, as quite often a 'gaseous vertebrate' conception of God (one that anthropomorphizes God and conceives of God as a kind of superhuman) comes dressed in metaphysical garb, which can make the

---

[12] The phrase is Ernst Häckel's and mentioned by Wittgenstein in CL 319.

[13] 'All that Frazer does is to make the practice plausible to those who think like him. It is very strange to present all these practices, in the end, so to speak, as foolishness. But it never does become plausible that people do all this out of sheer stupidity' (RFGB §1).

crudeness harder to spot. For example, the God of analytic theism is conceived as an all-powerful, all-knowing, all-good 'person without a body' – where a 'person without a body' is usually regarded in Cartesian manner as a purely 'mental substance'.[14] Here, the idea is that human beings have both a mind and a body – where, if you are a Cartesian (or neo-Cartesian), these words refer to distinct substances (or entities). Hence, if God is like a person but lacks a body, he comes out, on this view, as being a super-powerful 'mental substance', something very like a 'gaseous vertebrate'.

Such a 'gaseous vertebrate' conception seems clearly driven by Augustine's picture of language discussed earlier: the meaning of a word is the object it stands for. 'God', being a proper name, that is, the name of a person – but obviously not of a physical one with tendons and toenails – must, therefore, be the name of a disembodied one: a purely 'spiritual' being. In other words, the 'surface grammar' of the word 'God' tempts us to think that 'God' names a human-like object, when, really, Wittgenstein believes, the 'depth grammar' is quite different.

But how do we work out what the depth grammar is? In the same way as we would with any other word – by attending to the difference its employment makes in lived praxis:

> Really what I should like to say is that here too what is important is not the *words* you use or what you think while saying them, so much as the difference that they make at different points in your life. How do I know that two people mean the same when each says he believes in God? And just the same thing goes for the Trinity. Theology that insists on *certain* words & phrases & prohibits others, makes nothing clearer. (Karl Barth)
>
> It gesticulates with words, as it were, because it wants to say something & does not know how to express it. *Practice* gives the words their sense (CV 97e/85e).

What Wittgenstein seems to be saying here is that it is not possible to find out what someone means – or, indeed, whether two people mean the same – merely by looking at the words these people use. For they can use the *same words* and yet mean something completely different. Augustine's picture glosses over this important insight by insisting that all that matters to meaning is reference: as long as we have some idea of what the objects are that the words in question are supposed to refer to, we know what the words mean. But this, of course, is very simplistic. Not only is 'reference' itself a word in the language, which might not have a context-invariant use (i.e. 'reference' might mean slightly different things in different contexts), but knowing only that the word stands for some

---

[14] See, for example, Swinburne (2001, 2016) as a case *instar omnium*.

object does not give you the rules for the correct use of the word. This is why Wittgenstein spends so much time talking about ostensive definition at the beginning of PI. An ostensive definition will only teach me the rules for the correct use of a word if the overall role of the word in the language is already clear (PI §30) – that is, if I already know what a name is, for instance, and how it functions: 'When one shows someone the king in chess and says "This is the king", one does not thereby explain to him the use of this piece – unless he already knows the rules of the game except for this last point: the shape of the king' (PI §31).

Presumably, Wittgenstein is criticizing Barth (in the previous passage from CV) for merely insisting on a different form of words (Barth wanted to replace talk of a 'three person' God with the concept of God's *Seinsweisen* (ways of being)[15]), instead of clarifying the actual *use* of the word 'Trinity'. That is to say, Wittgenstein seems to think that banning one form of words, while allowing another, will not deepen one's understanding of the relevant concept, unless the new form of words makes a significant difference to the religious practice itself.[16] If it makes no difference which form of words is used, then these words are idle wheels: 'a wheel that can be turned though nothing else moves with it is not part of the mechanism' (PI §271).

1.4 Reception and Strategy

Although Wittgenstein's conception of religious belief has been enormously influential – both in philosophy as well as in theology[17] – it has also been subject to considerable distortion. In the contemporary literature, for example, Wittgenstein has variously been labelled a fideist (Nielsen, in Nielsen & Phillips, 2005), a non-cognitivist (Glock, 1995; Hyman, 2001) and a relativist of sorts (Kusch, 2011). What most of these views have in common is that they take for granted that the standard 'cognitive'/ 'non-cognitive' dichotomy is the only game in town: religious beliefs are either to be construed as straightforwardly 'factual' beliefs, whose content can be expressed in ordinary propositions (cognitivism), or religious beliefs

---

[15] See Barth (2003: 355).

[16] For a more charitable interpretation of what Barth might have been up to, see Schönbaumsfeld (in press).

[17] D. Z. Phillips is probably the first and most prominent proponent of a Wittgensteinian philosophy of religion (see, for example, Phillips, 2014 (first published 1965), 1988, 1993). Other major philosophical figures who have made good use of Wittgenstein's ideas on religious belief include Cyril Barrett (1991), John Cottingham (2009), Cora Diamond (2005), Peter Winch (1987, 1995), Stephen Mulhall (2001) and Hilary Putnam (1992). Prominent theologians influenced by Wittgenstein include Fergus Kerr (1986), Paul Holmer (2012), Andrew Moore (2003) and Rowan Williams (2014). Philosophers and theologians from other religious traditions have also engaged with Wittgenstein (see, for instance, Talal Asad (2020) and Eugene Borowitz (2006)).

are purely 'expressive' – that is to say, they express our attitudes to various things, but are entirely devoid of factual content (non-cognitivism).[18]

Such readings, however, are seriously at odds not just with what Wittgenstein says about religious belief but with much of his later philosophy. As should already be apparent from the overview previously offered, Wittgenstein's philosophy is in the business of challenging the orthodox categories and terms of engagement, so we shouldn't be surprised if Wittgenstein's actual view cannot be made to fit onto either side of a dichotomy that may well turn out to present us with a false picture of how to construe religious belief. Rather than cleaving to this false dichotomy, therefore, what I intend to show in the remaining sections is that what Wittgenstein offers us instead is an important 'third way'[19] of understanding religious belief – one that does not fall into the trap of either assimilating religious beliefs to ordinary empirical (or meta-empirical) beliefs or seeking to reduce them to the expression of certain attitudes or forms of life. For, on the reading that I offer, attitude and content are one – neither can be understood, or made sense of, in isolation from the other.

The strategy I adopt is as follows. Building on some of the themes already articulated, I aim to show how Wittgenstein's view undermines the following three misconceptions about religious belief:

(1) The word 'God' is the name of a super-empirical entity.
(2) It is possible to investigate whether God exists as one would investigate a scientific hypothesis or theory.
(3) The meaning of religious concepts can be understood in isolation from religious practice.

Clearly, all three claims are closely connected. Nonetheless, I will devote a separate section to each, showing why the notion is mistaken and what ramifications this has. In the penultimate section, I will address remaining objections to Wittgenstein's view, such as the 'incommensurability' charge and the

---

[18] Although there are scholars who have questioned this distinction (e.g. Clack, 1996; Burley 2018), the difficulty of extricating oneself from it can be seen in the fact that Clack (1996, 1999), for example, on the one hand criticizes the instrumentalist reductionism implicit in expressivism (Clack, 1996), but on the other hand ends ups forgetting his own lesson when he claims that Wittgenstein's later conception of religious belief implies atheism (Clack, 1999), as it gets rid of the metaphysical content of religion. The notion that the 'content' of religious belief can only be cashed out in metaphysical terms, and otherwise reduces to the expression of emotional attitudes or primitive reactions (Mackie, 1982; Clack, 1999; Schröder, 2007; Haldane 2007, 2008), is precisely the view that this book seeks to undermine. Also see Burley (2012, 2018) for a good critical discussion of Clack, and Burley (2008) for a response to Haldane.

[19] I first articulated such a conception in Schönbaumsfeld (2007).

thought that his conception implies a form of relativism. In Section 6, I offer a brief overall assessment.

2 The Grammar of 'God'

2.1 Introduction

In the *Lectures on Religious Belief*, which Wittgenstein held in Cambridge in 1938, he is reported as saying the following:

> The word 'God' is amongst the earliest learnt – pictures and catechisms, etc. But not the same consequences as with pictures of aunts. I wasn't shown [that which the picture pictured]. The word is used like a word representing a person. God sees, rewards, etc. 'Being shown all these things, did you understand what this word meant?' I'd say: 'Yes and no. I did learn what it didn't mean. I made myself understand. I could answer questions, understand questions when they were put in different ways – and in that sense could be said to understand.' If the question arises as to the existence of a god or God, it plays an entirely different role to that of the existence of any person or object I ever heard of. One said, had to say, that one believed in the existence, and if one did not believe, this was regarded as something bad. Normally if I did not believe in the existence of something no one would think there was anything wrong in this. (LC 59)[20]

In this passage, Wittgenstein seems to be saying the following four different, but inter-related, things:

(1) While pictures of aunts are representational in the sense that they provide a depiction of a person that one could also encounter independently of the picture, a 'picture' of God is not representational in the same sense.

(2) The word 'God' is used like a word representing a person, but, at the same time, it plays an entirely different role to that of the existence of any person or object Wittgenstein has ever heard of.

(3) The use of the word 'belief' also seems different: in the case of God, one had to say that one believed in him, whereas such a demand was not made in respect to any other kind of object.

(4) Wittgenstein hesitates to say whether he understands the word 'God' or not. He says that he did learn what the word didn't mean, and that he could answer various questions put to him.

In this section, I will examine each of these points in turn and explain how it contributes to an elucidation of the grammar of religious belief. This will also enable us to avoid a common misinterpretation of Wittgenstein's conception.

---

[20] Additional paragraphing removed.

2.2 Pictures of Aunts and Pictures of God

Similarly to what was established in Section 1, points 1–3 imply that Wittgenstein thinks that while the 'surface grammar' of the word 'God' is similar to that of an ordinary person – 'God sees and rewards' – the 'depth grammar' is actually quite different ('it plays an entirely different role to that of the existence of any person or object I ever heard of'). That is to say, in some respects, the word appears to function like a word representing a person, but then these similarities suddenly come to an end. In the case of being shown a picture of my aunt (point 1), I can, for example, ask myself whether this picture is a good likeness of the aunt I have seen in the flesh, what age my aunt was when she was photographed or painted, whether she still looks like she did in the picture, and so on. But none of these 'consequences' follow in the case of being shown a 'picture of God' – here it makes no sense to ask whether the picture is a 'good likeness' or whether it corresponds to the God I have 'seen'. Consequently, a 'picture of God' cannot play a representational role in the way that a picture of an aunt can. To think otherwise would be to be misled by the surface grammar into adopting the 'gaseous vertebrate' view mentioned in Section 1 – to believe that God is like a 'person without a body', who could, say, 'materialize' and then be 'depicted', if he felt like it. And here we could only understand what 'materialize' meant by imagining some occult process whereby a 'soul' or 'consciousness' gets 'transferred' into a body (which then has to be imagined as being created ad hoc and ex nihilo as well, so that, for instance, Michelangelo could paint it).

In speaking this way, we would again be duped by Augustine's picture and physical object language, for we seem to model what 'transferred' could mean in this context on physical object discourse – that is, on the idea of moving one object into another object. We imagine, for instance, that a soul or 'consciousness' is an 'immaterial' object that gets 'relocated' into a material one. But how can one make sense of the notion of 'relocating' or 'transferring' something 'immaterial' that has no physical boundaries? We appear to get into dreadful muddles if we think that it makes sense to construe the grammar of 'God' along 'gaseous vertebrate' lines.[21] This is why Wittgenstein says in the conversation with Rhees quoted in Section 1 that 'if you try to talk about God as you would talk about a human being, you are likely to come to talk nonsense, to ask nonsensical questions and so on' (Rhees, 2001: 413).

Relatedly, point 2 also seems to imply that when we speak of the 'existence' of God, these words cannot play the same role as they would were we to speak

---

[21] Many classical problems about God's omnipotence seem to be the result of such confusions – e.g. 'Can God create a stone too heavy for him to lift?' etc.

of the existence of tables and chairs, unicorns, or the Loch Ness monster. For while one could mount an expedition to try and find out whether some strange animal lives in a Scottish lake, there can be no such thing as mounting an expedition to 'find God'. Anyone who attempted to do such a thing would be considered very badly confused, if not crazy (like Nietzsche's 'madman', perhaps). What all of this shows is that the grammar of 'God' does not function like the grammar of a super-empirical object that one could, in principle, encounter if only one had the relevant faculties or equipment.

Neither does 'existence' appear to mean the same when applied to God as when we use it to speak of ordinary entities, for 'existence' is a temporal phenomenon that has duration: every existing thing can come into and go out of existence. But God, for religious believers, always is and always was. Kierkegaard's pseudonymous author, Climacus, puts it well: 'God does not exist, he is eternal' (*Concluding Unscientific Postscript* (CUP) 332). One might, anachronistically, call this a grammatical remark that determines the concept of 'God' more precisely. Since we know that Wittgenstein greatly admired Kierkegaard and was deeply influenced by his conception of religious belief, we should not be surprised by this congruence.[22] Compare, for example, what Climacus says in his other 'work', *Philosophical Fragments*, with a remark Wittgenstein makes in *Culture and Value*:

> God is not a name but a concept, and perhaps because of that his *essentia involvit existentiam* [essence involves existence] (Kierkegaard, 1981: 41).

> God's essence is said to guarantee his existence – what this really means is that what is at issue here is not the existence of some *thing* [*daß es sich um eine Existenz nicht handelt*; translation emended; emphasis added].
>
> For could one not equally say that the essence of colour guarantees its existence? As opposed, say, to the white elephant. For it really only means: I cannot explain what 'colour' is, what the word 'colour' means, without the help of a colour sample. So in this case there is no such thing as explaining 'what it *would* be like if colours *were* to exist'.
>
> And now we might say: There can be a description of what it would be like if there were gods on Olympus – but not: 'what it would be like if there were God'. And this determines the concept 'God' more precisely. (CV 94/82)

In other words, what both Climacus and Wittgenstein seem to be saying here is that 'God' cannot be the name of a super-empirical object or entity that might perhaps exist – and whose existence one would be required to demonstrate – as God, for religious believers, 'necessarily exists'. Furthermore, and contrary to

---

[22] See Schönbaumsfeld (2007) for an in-depth study of the extent of Kierkegaard's influence on Wittgenstein.

what Anselm and Descartes thought, neither philosopher believes that it makes sense to regard 'necessary existence' as a *kind* of existence. For God's 'existence' is not a 'superior' token of the same type, but categorically different. It is for this reason that Climacus says that 'God' is not a name but a concept; that God does not 'exist' but is eternal (timeless). Since God can neither come into, nor go out of, existence in the same way that ordinary, contingently existing things can start and cease to exist, to speak of 'necessary existence' is really a way of marking a categorial or grammatical distinction; it is not to attribute a strange 'property' to God. It is for these reasons that Wittgenstein says, 'what this [*essentia involvit existentiam*] really means is that what is at issue here is not the existence of some *thing*'.[23] The grammar of 'God' does not operate like the grammar of an ordinary empirical entity or thing, not even a super-powerful one.

This also helps to explain why Wittgenstein thinks that one could describe what it would be like if there were gods on Mount Olympus, but not what it would be like if there were such a thing as God. For the Greek gods – contrary to the God of Christianity, say – are essentially like human beings; they just happen to have more powers. Consequently, it makes sense to say that these beings have a domicile (Mount Olympus) and that one could, in principle, encounter them, if one happened to catch them there.[24] Since the grammar of 'God' functions quite differently, however, one cannot become aware of God in the way that one could become aware of a Greek god or of the Loch Ness monster, if these things happened to exist. For, in the latter cases, a 'direct' relation to these creatures is possible, but in the case of God it is not, since God is not an 'externality' in the sense that a policeman is (Kierkegaard, 1980: 80). Hence, one cannot relate to God in the way one would relate to something that could be directly perceivable (such as a unicorn or the Loch Ness monster, if there were such things), as God is, in principle (i.e. categorically), not directly perceivable.[25]

---

[23] This point gets lost in Peter Winch's translation of 'what is at issue here is not the existence of something', as the English 'something' could imply that something doesn't exist, rather than that what is at issue is not an *Existenz* (a thing/entity) (which is what the German means). For a discussion of what implications these points have for the ontological argument, see Schönbaumsfeld (2007: ch. 4).

[24] This does not imply that the Greeks must have thought that they could straightforwardly encounter the gods there – only that they are in principle perceivable in the sense that, in certain circumstances, one could interact with them as with a person.

[25] Even if a Christian believes that Jesus Christ is God, God is not directly perceivable. For, as Kierkegaard points out, Christ is the 'sign of contradiction' (i.e. it is not 'directly perceivable' that he is God). In this much, Christ is always 'incognito' – his divinity is only for the eyes of faith (see, for example, Kierkegaard, 1991: 97, 135). For further discussion, see Schönbaumsfeld (2007).

Early Wittgenstein was already anticipating something like this insight when he said: 'God does not manifest himself *in* the world' (TLP 6.432). That is to say, God's 'existence' (or non-existence) is not a super-empirical fact whose obtaining or not obtaining would register in an inventory of all that is the case in the world (if such an idea made sense), and, consequently, there is no such thing as describing what it 'would be like' if God were to exist. For the facts in the world remain the same, whether there is a God or not. To become aware of God's presence is, therefore, quite different from becoming aware of some strange object whose existence had so far escaped one's notice. In later Wittgenstein's words:

> Life can educate you to 'believing in God'. And *experiences* too are what do this but not visions, or other sense experiences, which show us 'the existence of this being', but, e.g. sufferings of various sorts. And they do not show us God as a sense experience does an object, nor do they give rise to *conjectures* about him. Experiences, thoughts, – life can force this concept on us. (CV 97/86)

When life forces the concept 'God' upon us, we experience a conversion – we are taught a new way of seeing and making sense of the world. In this respect, coming to believe in God is more similar to discovering new dimensions or novel aspects in something than like making an ontological discovery about an as-yet-unheard-of object. Wittgenstein's remarks on aspect-perception in PI provide a useful way of explaining what such a new 'way of seeing' might involve: 'I observe a face, and then suddenly notice its likeness to another. I *see* that it has not changed; and yet I see it differently. I call this experience "noticing an aspect"' (*Philosophy of Psychology, a Fragment* (PPF) §113; xi: 193). To notice an aspect, such as a likeness between two faces, is quite different from noticing an object's colour, for instance. For I could show you the colour by drawing the object with or without the colour, but I cannot show you the likeness between the two faces in the same way. When I draw the object with the different colour, I see that the object has changed; in the case of the likeness, I see that the object has *not* changed, and yet I see it differently. Something similar happens when I notice the 'rabbit-aspect' of the 'duck–rabbit' figure for the first time: the lines on the page remain unchanged, and yet I appear to see a 'different' drawing (see Figure 1).

In order to characterize what the difference in such cases consists in, rather than pointing to new visual features of the drawing, 'I would have explained by pointing to all sorts of pictures of rabbits, would perhaps have pointed to real rabbits, talked about their kind of life, or given an imitation of them' (PPF §120, xi: 194). In these cases, it is necessary to go 'beyond' the figure itself in order to explain what I see, as the rabbit aspect is not a property of the lines on the page in the same way that the

Figure 1 The duck–rabbit (from the 23 October 1892
issue of *Fliegende Blätter*), via Wikimedia Commons

shape of the 'appendages' or the colour of the dot are distinct material properties of the object drawn. It is for this reason that Wittgenstein says that 'seeing as' is not part of perception (PPF §137; xi: 197). Although in one sense we 'see' the drawing in a different way when we see the rabbit-aspect light up – which is why we continue to use the word 'see' – in another sense we don't see anything different, because the arrangement of marks on the page hasn't changed. So, what I'm noticing is not an additional visual feature of the object, but rather 'an internal relation between it and other objects' (PPF §248).

Learning to see internal relations between things, however, is not a matter of acquiring superior vision; it is much more akin to developing a new skill or conceptual capacity. This is why Wittgenstein says that 'only of someone *capable* of making certain applications of the figure with facility would one say that he saw it now *this* way, now *that* way' (PPF §222; xi: 208). For example, someone who had never seen any rabbits – either in real life, picture books, or on the Internet – would not be able to see the duck–rabbit as a rabbit. Neither would someone who had no experience with seeing two-dimensional pictures as representations of three-dimensional objects be able to see either the duck- or rabbit-aspect of the duck–rabbit figure. Instead, such a person would perhaps only be able to see what we see in an abstract drawing. Wittgenstein calls the inability to see 'something as something' 'aspect-blindness' (PPF §257; xi: 213). This is not a matter of having defective perceptual organs, but more akin to a lack of imagination or the absence of what, in another context, we call a 'musical ear' (PPF §260; xi: 214).

If we apply these thoughts to our previous discussion regarding belief in God, the implications are the following. Just as we don't learn to see the rabbit-aspect of the duck–rabbit figure by discovering any additional, purely visual features of the figure, so we don't come to believe in God by discovering a new, super-powerful entity in the world. This is why early Wittgenstein said that God does not manifest himself in the world. The states of affairs within the world stay the same, but one's whole way of looking at the world is transformed. The world, to speak with early Wittgenstein, 'waxes' (or 'wanes') as a whole, 'as if by accession [or loss] of meaning' (Wittgenstein, 1984: 5.7.1916).[26]

To be able to see the world in this transformed manner requires (hard) work on oneself and one's way of seeing things. Early Wittgenstein thought, for instance, that in order for religious meaning to be possible, one needed to renounce the comforts of the world; to practise what Kierkegaard calls infinite resignation.[27] Later Wittgenstein realizes that consciousness of sin and open-ness to the possibility of salvation are also necessary for truly *Christian* religious belief:

> Christianity is not a doctrine, not, I mean, a theory about what has happened & will happen to the human soul, but a description of something that actually takes place in human life. For 'recognition of sin' is an actual occurrence & so is despair & so is redemption through faith. Those who speak of it [. . .] are simply describing what has happened to them; whatever gloss someone may want to put on it! (CV 32/28)

In other words, Wittgenstein agrees with Kierkegaard that Christianity is an existence-communication, not a set of propositions about the antics of gaseous vertebrates. Christians are called to exist in the truth as lived out by Christ, the paradigm or pattern, not to add a new ontological belief to their philosophical system. For Christ did not come to bring speculative knowledge about God into the world, but in order to offer the promise of redemption, and this is an ethical category, not a theoretical (metaphysical) one. This is why Kierkegaard says that truth, in the sense in which Christ is the truth, 'is not a sum of statements, not a definition etc., but a life' (Kierkegaard, 1991: 205). Wittgenstein says something very similar:

> It appears to me as though a religious belief could only be (something like) passionately committing oneself to a system of reference [of coordinates][28] [*Bezugssystem/Koordinatensystem*]. Hence, although it's belief, it's really a way of living, or a way of judging [beurteilen] life. Passionately taking up *this* conception[29] [*Auffassung*]. (CV 73/64)

---

[26] See Schönbaumsfeld (2018a) for further discussion.

[27] For more on this, see Schönbaumsfeld (2018a).

[28] The 1998 edition has 'system of coordinates', with 'system of reference' as an alternative; the 1977 edition has 'system of coordinates'.

[29] Winch has 'interpretation', which does not strike me as a good translation of 'Auffassung' in this context.

Read the wrong way, this could make it sound like Wittgenstein is saying that Christianity requires commitment to a 'doctrineless' form of life,[30] where all that matters is that you live a certain way, rather than that you hold certain kinds of belief. Although this interpretation is, unfortunately, very common,[31] it is false, for Wittgenstein is not saying, in this passage, that religious belief is not *belief* (Glaube). Rather, he is saying that *although* it's belief, it's *also* a way of living. The original German makes this more evident than the not terribly good English translation that seems to oppose 'belief' and 'way of living' to each other, whereas the German reads: 'Also obgleich es *Glaube* ist, doch eine Art des Lebens', which carries the implication that religious belief is *both* belief *and* way of life. In other words, the word 'belief' functions differently in religious discourse than in contexts where it just means 'intellectual assent to a proposition', for example. This chimes with Wittgenstein's point 3, mentioned at the beginning of this section, and elaborated further in the following paragraph: 'There is this extraordinary use of the word "believe". One talks of believing and at the same time one doesn't use "believe" as one does ordinarily. You might say (in the normal use): "You only believe-oh well . . ."' (LC 59–60).

That is to say, if Wittgenstein is right that the grammar of 'God' shows that this word is not the name of a super-empirical entity, then neither is 'belief in God' constituted by assent to the proposition 'God exists' – where this is taken to mean something like 'a gaseous vertebrate exists'. For not only does the word 'God' not function in this way (in 'belief in God'), neither does the word 'belief' operate in the same manner as it does in ordinary discourse: in a religious context, 'to believe' has very strong ethical implications; in ordinary discourse, it does not. As Wittgenstein pointed out in the passage quoted at the start of this section, not believing in God was considered to be something bad, whereas not believing in the existence of some ordinary empirical thing (black swans, say) carried no moral censure.

The reason for this difference must surely be that whether or not one can believe in God reveals something about oneself, and the kind of person one is (or could be capable of becoming), whereas mere intellectual assent to a proposition – for example, 'black swans exist' – does not, in the same way, depend on one's spiritual or moral capacities (although it may depend on one's intellectual integrity, which could make one more or less prone to accepting

---

[30] See, for example, Nielsen, in Nielsen & Phillips (2005: 116) and Hyman (2001: 7).

[31] See, e.g., Clack (1999), Hyman (2001), Graham (2014), McCutcheon (2001) and Schröder (2007).

how things actually are). As Kierkegaard says: 'Offence or faith; it is your heart that must be disclosed' (Kierkegaard, 1991: 97).

Consequently, it is not that Wittgenstein is saying that belief in God reduces to a 'content-free' attitude or way of life. Rather, the way one lives shows which 'system of reference' (moral or religious) one is committed to. Belief in God is not, therefore, an isolated intellectual belief – it is not mere assent to the existence of a 'God of the philosophers' – but is exemplified in one's passionate commitment to a whole way of living and thinking.[32]

If this is right, then Wittgenstein rejects what one might call a 'factorization' model of religious belief.[33] That is to say, in order to understand religious faith, one cannot separate 'form' (religious way of life; religious attitudes) from 'content' (doctrinal claims), as the form itself contributes to and transforms the meaning of the content. In this sense, form and content are one. The attempt to separate the two distorts the beliefs, however faithfully one reports the 'doctrine' (say by 'rote-reciting' the Creeds (as Kierkegaard might say[34])). I take it that this is why Wittgenstein hesitates to say whether he managed to learn what 'God' means by being shown pictures and given the catechism (point 4 above). Wittgenstein says that he learnt what the word didn't mean, which, perhaps, indicates that he managed to understand the difference in grammar between talk of God and that of any ordinary person or object, but the implication remains that this is somehow not sufficient. Further clues as to the reasons for this can be found in an earlier lecture in the same series:

> There are, for instance, these entirely different ways of thinking first of all – which needn't be expressed by one person saying one thing, another person another thing.
>
> What we call believing in a Judgement Day or not believing in a Judgement Day – The expression of belief may play an absolutely minor role.
>
> If you ask me whether or not I believe in a Judgement Day, in the sense in which religious people have belief in it, I wouldn't say: 'No. I don't believe there will be such a thing.' It would seem to me utterly crazy to say this.
>
> And then I give an explanation: 'I don't believe in ... ', but then the religious person never believes what I describe. (LC 55)

In the first two paragraphs of this passage, Wittgenstein says that the religious believer and the non-believer think entirely differently, but that this difference needn't show up in the form of words employed by them. Again, the implication seems to be that the different ways of 'assessing life' that characterize these

---

[32] This is much more similar to acceptance of a 'hinge framework' than it is like commitment to a set of ordinary propositional beliefs. See Section 3 for further discussion.

[33] For more on this, see Schönbaumsfeld (2014).

[34] For further discussion, see Schönbaumsfeld (2007).

different ways of thinking are not a matter of words alone, and can't be understood merely by attending to what these people *say*. In this much, the difference between them cannot be characterized as a difference in opinion (mere disagreement about a claim), for if religious believer and non-believer differed only in opinion, then it would be possible for the one just to affirm or deny what the other says. But Wittgenstein appears to reject this when he says that 'the religious person never believes what I describe'. In other words, Wittgenstein seems to be saying that although he could give a 'description' of a belief in a Judgement Day, the religious believer would nonetheless not believe what Wittgenstein describes.

I take it that the reason why Wittgenstein says that the religious person would not believe what Wittgenstein describes is that all that Wittgenstein can do is to give a kind of code-like paraphrase of the form of words the believer uses, without being able fully to appreciate how this belief informs, and makes a difference to, the believer's life. For, in order to be able to do that, Wittgenstein himself would have to be able to live completely differently:

> I am reading: '& no man can say that Jesus is the Lord, but by the Holy Ghost.' – And it is true: I cannot call him *Lord*; because that says [absolutely] nothing [*gar nichts*][35] to me. I could call him 'the paragon', 'God' even or rather: I can understand it when he is so called; but I cannot utter the word 'Lord' meaningfully. *Because I do not believe* that he will come to judge me; because *that* says nothing to me. And it could only say something to me if I were to live *quite* differently. (CV 38/33)

Wittgenstein, in this remark, seems to reject the idea that words communicate something merely by imparting some minimal 'cognitive' content that one could strip away from, or milk out of, the believer's 'belief-attitude'. Rather, the implication again appears to be that the content is itself determined by the attitude (and way of life) and vice versa. This is why Wittgenstein says that he could only utter the word 'Lord' with meaning if he lived completely differently. For a different life implies a different practice, which, in turn, implies a different use for the same words (signs) and, hence, a different sense. So, while Wittgenstein and the religious believer are using the same words (the same signs), these words, Wittgenstein suggests, symbolize in an entirely different way in the life of the practising believer than they do outside of that context. Consequently, although Wittgenstein can use the words 'Last Judgement' and say that he doesn't believe in it, he thinks the religious believer never believes what Wittgenstein describes.

---

[35] The 1977 translation lacks 'absolutely', which seems preferable to me. The addition of 'absolutely' is an overstated rendition of 'gar nichts'.

2.3 Not a 'Normal' Controversy

Wittgenstein's conception appears to imply that believer and non-believer cannot contradict each other. As Wittgenstein himself goes on to point out in the next sentence following the passage from LC already quoted: 'I can't say. I can't contradict that person' (LC 55). Interestingly, Wittgenstein's interlocutor then goes on to offer a reason for this, which Wittgenstein is also not happy with: 'You might say: "Well, if you can't contradict him, that means you don't understand him. If you did understand him, then you might." That again is Greek to me. My normal technique of language leaves me. I don't know whether to say they understand one another or not' (LC 55). In line with the interpretation offered in the previous subsection, Wittgenstein hesitates to say whether believer and non-believer understand one another or not, because, in one sense, they do understand one another – as previously elaborated, Wittgenstein understands the words 'God', 'Last Judgement' and so on – but in another sense they don't, for Wittgenstein doesn't understand how a *life* with such a concept is possible, or how one would go about acquiring the qualities of heart that would make it so. This is why Wittgenstein says 'These controversies look quite different from any normal controversies. Reasons look entirely different from normal reasons. They are, in a way, quite inconclusive'[36] (LC 56).

Wittgenstein thinks, I believe, that this is not a 'normal controversy', as normal controversies are like differences in opinion: I affirm the same claim that the other denies. But, as we have already seen, Wittgenstein does not think that, in the religious case, it's as simple as that. Believer and non-believer seem not just words, but *worlds* apart. Wittgenstein, therefore, rejects the interlocutor's suggestion, because he is taking it that the interlocutor believes that as soon as the meaning of the words is clarified, we are back to having a 'normal' disagreement again.

In Section 3, we will encounter some more reasons why Wittgenstein believes that we are not dealing with a 'normal controversy' here: the role that evidence does (or does not) play, and the implications it has, if we make religious belief 'a question of science' (LC 57). This will enable us to understand why Wittgenstein thinks that, in respect to religious belief, 'reasons look entirely different from normal reasons', and, hence, why he says that the difference between the believer and the non-believer is not best characterized as a 'normal controversy' – an ordinary disagreement about certain matters of fact.

---

[36] Additional paragraphing removed.

3 Making it a Question of Science

3.1 Introduction

In the passage immediately following the one we discussed at the end of Section 2, Wittgenstein says:

> The point is that if there were evidence, this would in fact destroy the whole business. Anything that I normally call evidence wouldn't in the slightest influence me. Suppose, for instance, we knew people who foresaw the future; make forecasts for years and years ahead; and they described some sort of a Judgement Day. Queerly enough, even if there were such a thing, and even if it were more convincing than I have described [. . .] belief in this happening wouldn't be at all a religious belief. (LC 56)

In this paragraph, Wittgenstein seems to be making the following three points:

(1) The availability of evidence would destroy the very idea of religious belief.
(2) Ordinary evidence would have no impact on Wittgenstein acquiring (or not acquiring) a religious belief.
(3) An ordinary forecast that predicted some sort of 'Judgement Day' would not be a religious belief.

In this section, I will explain why Wittgenstein holds each of these three views and what implications they have for philosophers, theologians and ordinary religious believers who want to make religion 'a question of science' (LC 57). This will also provide us with further reasons why Wittgenstein believes that disagreements about religious belief are not 'normal controversies'. In the final subsection, I will critically discuss the idea that Wittgenstein is propounding a form of 'fideism'.

3.2 A Confusion of the Spheres

Let's start with point 1 and the question of why Wittgenstein thinks that the availability of evidence would 'destroy the whole business'. From the context, it seems clear that by 'evidence' Wittgenstein means 'empirical evidence': He speaks, for instance, of forecasts, of probabilities (LC 57) and of scientific hypotheses (LC 57). Consequently, what Wittgenstein appears to be saying is that the availability of empirical evidence would destroy religious belief – quite ironic, given how many atheists lament precisely its absence!

So, what does Wittgenstein mean? Why does he think that the availability of empirical evidence, rather than being welcome, would in fact destroy every-thing? I take it that the reasons for this are connected to the grammatical differences between God-talk and discourse about ordinary entities that we discussed in Section 2. That is to say, if there could be such a thing as evidence for the 'existence of God', then God would be an in principle perceivable (observable) entity whose existence one could infer from empirical grounds such as, say, from footprints or the behaviour of light. This would be to treat the concept of 'God' analogously to the idea of the Loch Ness monster, for example, or to a distant planet. On such a conception, there would only be a quantitative difference between God and a human being (i.e. the former would only differ from the latter in respect to how much more of certain properties – such as powers – this entity has); there would not be a *qualitative* distinction.

But to conflate the grammar of God with that of a bodiless super-person constitutes, to speak with Kierkegaard, a 'confusion of the spheres' (*Book on Adler* (BA) 5). For, as we have already seen, the concept of God does not operate like the name of a gaseous vertebrate, whose presence one could establish by scientific means. Consequently, it makes no sense to think that one could find information about God in a geography book (Kierkegaard, 1991: 29) or make him 'observable' by means of an electron microscope.

In this respect, there is also no similarity between God and unobservable entities in science (*pace* Swinburne (2001, 2016) and others who would dispute this). Theological realists (or philosophical theists) who wish to transfer the grammar of observation talk in science to God are, therefore, and as Moore correctly points out, guilty of making a 'category mistake' (Moore, 2003: 65). What is more, the putative analogy between unobservable entities in science and an 'unobservable' God collapses into incoherence, precisely because God is necessarily (i.e. in principle) unobservable:

> If they [the theological realists] wish to uphold the theological side of the analogy (i.e. that God is unobservable in principle), they will have to affirm that scientifically unobservable entities are also unobservable in principle. Yet this denies the principle of scientific realism that the observable/unobservable dichotomy is false, so the analogy collapses on philosophical grounds. On the other hand, if theological realists concede the scientific realist principle and persist in upholding an analogy with reference in the philosophy of science, they will have to contradict their theological principle that God is necessarily unobservable, and so they will be led to affirm that God is in principle observable. The analogy will then collapse on theological grounds. (Moore, 2003: 65)

The dilemma that Moore presents is fatal, in other words, because it neither makes sense to say that God could, in principle, be observable, nor that unobservable scientific entities are in principle unobservable, since, in the empirical realm, this would be tantamount to saying that these entities are fictitious (i.e. that there are, in fact, no such entities). Consequently, there is no coherent analogy between a necessarily unobservable God and contingently unobservable entities in science.

This also helps us to understand Wittgenstein's point about the availability of evidence. If it were possible to acquire evidence for the existence of God, then this possibility would make God only contingently unobservable – like an electron that could, in principle, be made visible – and this is at odds with the grammar of 'God', which is not the grammar of an elusive spatio-temporal particle. In short, a belief in a god whose existence one could empirically demonstrate would not be a religious belief, just an ordinary empirical belief that a strange new entity exists.

The same goes for treating a belief in a 'Judgement Day' like an ordinary empirical forecast (point 3) – this, too, would not be a religious belief, but something more akin to the kind of prediction a futurologist might make. This is why Wittgenstein says, 'That is partly why you don't get in religious controversies, the form of controversy where one person is sure of the thing, and the other says : "Well, possibly"'(LC 56). The religious person, who is sure that there will be a Judgement Day, is not treating his belief as an empirical prediction that might be provable or falsifiable by future evidence. Consequently, he also doesn't think that such an 'event' is 'possible' – that is, that it possesses a certain degree of empirical likelihood – as his belief does not depend on empirical probabilities at all. For if taken to be continuous with ordinary empirical beliefs, his belief in a Judgement Day would be conditional on better evidence becoming available, and such an idea makes no sense in the religious case. This is why Wittgenstein thinks that those who said, 'Well, possibly it may happen and possibly not', 'would be on an entirely different plane' (LC 56). That is to say, those who said the latter would treat their belief as a normal forecast for which there is a certain amount of probability, whereas religious believers do not treat their belief in that way. Consequently, it is not accidental that in religious discourse words other than 'belief' are used to mark this difference: 'dogma' and 'faith'. Wittgenstein says, 'We don't talk about hypothesis, or about high probability. Nor about knowing' (LC 57). So, when we do employ the word 'belief' in religion, its grammar is different from the way the word is used in science and ordinary empirical discourse.

The 'controversy' between someone who believes in a Judgement Day in the religious sense and someone who understands this as an ordinary – if outlandish – empirical prediction is not, therefore, a 'normal controversy'; not, that is, one that could be settled by way of appeal to a set of common criteria. For the religious person and the non-believer are 'on an entirely different plane'. This is why Wittgenstein says that the religious believer never believes what Wittgenstein describes. Wittgenstein, qua non-believer, construes a belief in a Judgement Day as something akin to a strange empirical belief, while, at the same time, being aware that this is not what the religious person means, as the believer does not treat his belief like an ordinary forecast.

3.3 Science and Superstition

Naturally, Wittgenstein is aware that there are religious believers who make their beliefs 'a question of science':

> Father O'Hara is one of those people who make it a question of science.
>
> Here we have people who treat this evidence in a different way. They base things on evidence which taken in one way would seem exceedingly flimsy. They base enormous things on this evidence. Am I to say they are unreasonable? I wouldn't call them unreasonable.
>
> I would say, they are certainly not *reasonable*, that's obvious. (LC 57–8)

Father O'Hara was a professor of physics and mathematics at Heythrop College, London, who participated in a BBC debate about science and religion in the 1930s, and who thought that recent developments in relativity theory and quantum mechanics provided evidence for the existence of God. In other words, O'Hara is 'one of those people who make it a question of science', as he thinks that belief in God is similar to a scientific hypothesis that can be corroborated or falsified by empirical (or theoretical) evidence. A more recent example of someone with the same tendency would be Richard Swinburne.[37]

Of course, if someone holds that religious beliefs are to be assessed by the 'modern scientific criteria' (Swinburne, 2001: 3), they must be prepared to hold their beliefs to the same exacting standards of empirical corroboration and falsification as employed in science. And this seems to cause a problem for religion, as religious believers will then have to be construed as basing 'enormous things' on evidence that taken in one way – namely, the scientific, empirical way – will 'seem exceedingly flimsy'. Such 'enormous things' might, for example, be forgoing all pleasures for the sake of one's beliefs, and hence would involve a very dramatic change of life. If religious beliefs are to be treated and assessed like scientific ones, we will, therefore, end up with a significant mismatch between the amount of evidence available for these beliefs and the radical self-transformation that these beliefs require of one. It is for these reasons that Kierkegaard's Climacus thinks that basing your spiritual salvation on empirical approximation (empirical probabilities) is comical:

---

[37] See, in particular, Swinburne (2001: 9). For an extensive critique of Swinburne's position, see Schönbaumsfeld (2007).

> If the historical aspect of the Creed (that it is from the apostles etc.) is to be decisive, then every iota must be infinitely insisted upon, and since this can be attained only *approximando*, the individual finds himself in the contradiction of [...] wanting to tie his eternal happiness to it and not being able to do so because the approximation is never finished [...] The individual is tragic because of his passion and comic because of staking it on an approximation.
>
> (CUP 43)

In other words, if historical accuracy is required in order for Christian religious belief to be possible, then the Creed or the Gospels need to be subjected to the same vetting procedures as ordinary historical documents. Since no absolute certainty regarding such documents can ever be attained, however, and the vetting procedures can always throw up new, hitherto unconsidered evidence, the process is also never finished. Consequently, the believer who wants to base his belief on the historical evidence is in the unfortunate position of having to base an 'enormous' life decision on something that can only ever be an approximation in the sense that it is always subject to falsification by future experience. Hence, a mismatch arises because the extraordinary commitment of faith appears to require passionate, 'subjective' certainty or conviction, but the 'objective', scientific or historical point of view can only ever give one conditional truth (approximation/probability). So, basing the former on the latter is incongruous, and this gives rise to the comic.

Wittgenstein clearly has something like this point in mind when he says in the opening passage that 'anything that one would normally call evidence, wouldn't in the slightest influence me' (point 2 above). He also seems to agree with Kierkegaard's Climacus that Christianity does not rest on an ordinary historic basis:

> It has been said that Christianity rests on an historic basis.
>
> It has been said a thousand times by intelligent people that indubitability is not enough in this case. Even if there is as much evidence as for Napoleon. Because the indubitability wouldn't be enough to make me change my whole life.
>
> It doesn't rest on an historic basis in the sense that the ordinary belief in historic facts could serve as a foundation.
>
> Here we have a belief in historic facts different from a belief in ordinary historic facts. Even, they are not treated as historical, empirical, propositions.
>
> Those people who had faith didn't apply the doubt which would ordinarily apply to *any* historical propositions. Especially propositions of a time long past, etc. (LC 57)

Wittgenstein appears to be making two main points in this passage. First, that even indubitability would not be enough to make one change one's whole life; second, that the way the 'historic facts' figure in Christian faith is not how they are treated in ordinary (historical) empirical propositions, as, among other things, 'people who had faith didn't apply the doubt' that would ordinarily be applied to any historical claim. I will take the second point first.

Although, as Wittgenstein says in another passage from CV, Christianity offers us a historical narrative, Christianity is not based on a historical truth, in the sense that faith depends on the historical accuracy of the Gospels' claims.[38] For even if the Gospels could be shown to be completely accurate in respect to the people depicted etc., the events they speak of are, to a large extent, not the kind of events that could admit of a historical investigation at all. No historian ever investigates, for instance, whether a miracle has occurred or a person has been resurrected, since no empirical investigation could ever show (or not show) that such things have happened (or not). For a miracle is not just an ordinary, albeit highly improbable, event, but something categorically at odds with our ordinary ways of looking at the world. In this respect, one could say that talk of miracles is not an available move in the 'game' of historical or scientific enquiry.[39] If it were just like an ordinary, but very unlikely, event, such as a lottery win, say, then we could assign probability values to it.

To think that the latter is possible, however, betrays not just a qualitative (grammatical) confusion; the attempt would also founder on a whole host of other problems. Not only would we have to treat religious beliefs as beliefs about the behaviour of gaseous vertebrates and occult processes, but in so doing, we would also require responses to the following questions: (1) According to which criteria would we be able to assign probability values to 'supernatural' events, such as the resurrection of Christ, say, or the existence of the universe (as proponents of design arguments, such as Swinburne (Swinburne, 2001, 2016), want to maintain)? We have no experience of supernatural events on the basis of which a comparison with natural events could be made, such that we could say, for example, that 'supernatural event A' is more likely (probable) to occur than 'natural event B' or, indeed, that 'supernatural event A' is more likely to occur

---

[38] Nonetheless, if it could be proven beyond any reasonable doubt that there had never been a person like Jesus Christ (i.e. if no historical Jesus had existed at all), then that would be problematic. Exactly what the historical Jesus was like, however, does not greatly affect faith, since it is in any case impossible to make an inference from Jesus's historical characteristics to whether or not he was divine.

[39] This should not be read as implying that science, history or religion are distinct and self-contained 'language-games' (such a notion would be a gross oversimplification). Rather, Wittgenstein often uses the term 'language-game' as an object of comparison – i.e. to point to important differences in the context of use of a concept (which is what I am doing here too). See, for example, PI §130: 'Our clear and simple language-games are not preliminary studies for a future regimentation of language – as it were, first approximations, ignoring friction and air resistance. Rather, the language-games stand there as *objects of comparison* which, through similarities and dissimilarities, are meant to throw light on features of our language.'

than 'supernatural event C'. (2) What criteria or processes would enable us to tell at which point it becomes 'likely' that a natural event (or set of events) has a 'supernatural' cause rather than a merely natural one? Can one quantify oneself into a qualitative distinction? That is, can one make the leap from improbable 'natural' causes to *probable* 'supernatural' ones? This seems absurd. (3) Is it possible, by ordinary empirical or scientific means, to establish that there are supernatural events or causes in the first place?[40]

Since the prospects of responding to these problems in a satisfactory manner, compatible with the 'modern scientific criteria', appear to be dim, the attempt to make religion a 'question of science' seems doomed to failure. Consequently, it is not surprising that Kierkegaard says:

> To make Christianity probable is the same as to falsify it. Indeed, what is it that atheists want? Oh, they want to make Christianity probable. That is, they are well aware that if they can only get Christianity's qualitative extravagance tricked into the fussy officiousness of probability – then it is all over with Christianity. (BA 39)

In other words, if the Christian religious claims are to be treated no differently than ordinary empirical, or super-empirical propositions, then it is all over with Christianity, as by these lights, and as Wittgenstein says, 'if this is religious belief, then it's all superstition' (LC 59). That is to say, Wittgenstein believes that making religion 'a question of science', far from putting it onto a more 'secure' footing, thereby succeeds only in turning it into superstition – into a form of false science that one shouldn't, with a good conscience, buy into. This is why he says, 'What seems to me ludicrous about O'Hara is his making it appear to be reasonable', when, according to Wittgenstein, it would be more correct to say that 'they [the religious believers] don't treat this as a matter of reasonability' (LC 58).

Wittgenstein is not saying, then, that religious believers are *unreasonable*, but rather that religious beliefs (if not construed superstitiously) are neither reason-able nor unreasonable, as they are not rival scientific theories (for taken as such, they would come out 'ludicrous'). Consequently, Wittgenstein is not siding with the militant atheists or with people like Nielsen (Nielsen & Phillips, 2005), who want to debunk religious beliefs as irrational. One of the main points of criticism that Wittgenstein levels at the anthropologist Frazer, for example, is precisely that he wants to reduce religious beliefs to a form of false (or bizarre) science, and Wittgenstein regards this as point-missing:

---

[40] All of this implies the failure of cosmological and design arguments that claim that a supernatural cause is more 'likely' than a natural one for the existence of the universe. See Schönbaumsfeld (2018b) for further discussion.

> Frazer's representation of human magical and religious notions is unsatisfac-
> tory: it makes these notions appear as *mistakes*. Was Augustine mistaken,
> then, when he called on God on every page of the *Confessions*? But – one
> might say – if he was not in error, then surely was the Buddhist saint – or
> whoever else – whose religion expresses entirely different notions. But none
> of them was in error except where he was putting forth a theory. (RFGB §1)

That is to say, it is only if religious belief is construed as analogous to, or as
a rival of, a scientific theory that Wittgenstein thinks it makes sense to regard
such beliefs as errors. For then, as we have seen, they are false science, and fail
by the very criteria they have misguidedly wanted to appropriate.

Since we have already seen that so to construe religious beliefs is tantamount
to a 'confusion of the spheres', however, we need to pay closer attention to the
actual grammar of religious practices. This will show us, Wittgenstein thinks,
that 'here [in Christian religious belief] we have a belief in historic facts
different from a belief in ordinary historic facts' (LC 57). In other words, just
as the concept of 'belief' functions differently in religion than it does in ordinary
discourse, so Christian belief in 'historic facts' is qualitatively different from
belief in ordinary historical propositions:

> Christianity is not based on a historical truth, but presents us with
> a (historical) narrative & says: now believe! But not, believe this report
> [*Nachricht*] with the belief that is appropriate to a historical report, – but
> rather: believe through thick & thin & you can do this only as the outcome
> [*Resultat*] of a life. *Here you have a message!* [*Nachricht*] – *don't treat it as
> you would another historical message!* Make a *quite* different place for it in
> your life. (CV 37/32)

Although it is, of course, possible to lose one's faith, religious belief is not like
intellectual belief – it is not characterized by mere assent (or failure to assent) to
a proposition that is independently formulable and assessable by anyone (as
a scientific or historical proposition would be). Rather, a genuine religious
believer structures their entire life around these narratives, something that
would be inappropriate in the case of a scholar of history who must, in principle,
always be prepared to accept new evidence when it comes to light. But were
a religious believer to say, 'I believe in Jesus Christ until contrary evidence
becomes available', they would not be regarded as suitably open-minded, but as
guilty of a serious misunderstanding.

If this is right, then ordinary empirical evidence is not germane to the
question of whether or not one should acquire a religious belief. For such
evidence can neither justify nor undermine religious faith, since whatever it is
that such evidence is evidence for, it bypasses what the (non-superstitious)
believer believes. As Wittgenstein says, 'The best scientific evidence is just

nothing' (LC 56). And this is so, not only because it is not possible to quantify oneself into faith (CUP 11) (*pace* Father O'Hara, Swinburne et. al.), but also because empirical (or theoretical) evidence is not of the right kind to effect a self-transformation. In order fundamentally to change my life and to become a new person, I need, as Climacus tells us, to be engaged on a 'subjective', ethico-religious level, not an 'objective' one, where it is a matter of weighing up probabilities, or of following a set of edicts: Faith is first-personal, science (or historical scholarship) is not. A passage from CV, written in 1946, makes this clear:

> Amongst other things Christianity says, I believe, that sound doctrines are all useless. That you have to change your *life*. (Or the *direction* of your life.)
>
> That all wisdom is cold; & that you can no more use it for setting your life to rights, than you can forge iron when it is *cold*.
> For a sound doctrine need not *seize* you; you can follow it, like a doctor's prescription. – But here you have to be seized & turned around by something . . . Once turned round, you must *stay* turned round.
> Wisdom is passionless. By contrast Kierkegaard calls faith a *passion*.
>
> (CV 61/53)

Here, again, Wittgenstein is not saying that Christianity is not a doctrine in the sense that it has no conceptual content, but rather that it is not a doctrine in the sense of providing one with a recipe (or prescription) for how to live. For it is only possible to stay 'turned round' by becoming a new person – by, as it were, undergoing an ethical transformation – not by making some adjustments to one's intellectual beliefs, upon which some modifications of behaviour might (or might not) follow.

3.4 Hostile Reactions

Wittgenstein's critique of scientism and evidentialism (the view that religious belief does, or must, rest on evidence in the way that scientific (or other) theories do) in religion has led to some surprisingly hostile reactions, even from philosophers generally sympathetic to Wittgenstein's overall vision (see, in particular, Hyman (2001) and Nielsen (Nielsen & Phillips, 2005)). Here, for example, is Hyman:

> If a religious belief is something like a passionate commitment to a system of reference – as opposed to a passionate commitment to the truth of an empirical proposition – then a religious belief cannot be *true* or *false*. And Wittgenstein held that religious beliefs cannot be *reasonable* or *unreasonable* either, if that means that they can or cannot be justified. (Hyman, 2001: 6)

> The epistemological corollary, that religious beliefs are immune from rational
> criticism and incapable of receiving rational support, has the interesting
> consequence that, as Wittgenstein said, 'if Christianity is the truth, then all
> the philosophy about it is false' (CV, p.83), but it has little else to recommend
> it (Hyman, 2001:10).

The view that Wittgenstein believes that religious beliefs are immune to rational
criticism and incapable of receiving rational support has come to be known as
'Wittgensteinian Fideism'. Nielsen first coined the phrase in the 1960s, in response
to the writings of Peter Winch, but D. Z. Phillips' Wittgenstein-inspired philosophy
of religion was subsequently predominantly tarred with this brush.[41] In this section,
I will examine the question of whether Wittgenstein's contention that religious
belief is neither reasonable nor unreasonable entails an objectionable form of
fideism (as Hyman and Nielsen believe). I will argue that to think it does stems
from a misunderstanding of Wittgenstein's method and a failure to grasp that
Wittgenstein is challenging the familiar terms of engagement.

So, let's start by looking at the assumptions (explicit or implicit) that someone who thinks that Wittgenstein is a dubious fideist tends to make:[42]

(a) The grammar of 'God' is not relevantly different from that of a super-
powerful gaseous vertebrate. Consequently, religious beliefs are straightforward existential commitments to strange empirical, or super-empirical,
entities and their antics.

(b) Religious beliefs must, therefore, be substantiated in ordinary ways by
appeal to 'neutral' evidence that anyone can understand. In short, it must
be possible to prove, or, at the very least, make probable, that God exists,
before one can rationally commit oneself to a religious life.

(c) A 'passionate commitment to a system of reference', on the other hand,
excludes commitment to the truth of a proposition, and, in this much, is
tantamount to affirming that no rational evaluation of religious beliefs is
possible.

(d) To reject (a) and (b) is to espouse fideism.

The first thing to say in response to these moves, and in particular the conclusion
(d), is that they beg the question against Wittgenstein's whole way of proceeding. For, as we have already seen in Sections 1 and 2 (as well as Sections 3.1–
3.3), Wittgenstein gives us good reasons to doubt that the grammar of God

---

[41] See their most recent exchange in Nielsen & Phillips (2005), which also contains all the original
papers from the 1960s that started the debate; also see the entry on 'fideism' in the *Stanford
Encyclopaedia of Philosophy* (Amesbury, 2005/2022).

[42] I leave open whether Hyman or Nielsen (or anyone else making the same charge) are *explicitly*
committed to these claims.

functions like the grammar of a gaseous vertebrate that one must show exists, much as one would have to produce evidence for the Loch Ness monster, if belief in its existence were to count as rational. Consequently, Mulhall (2001) is right to insist against Hyman that:

> [if] no one can so much as understand what a belief in God's existence amounts to without grasping the location of that concept in the grammatical network of religious concepts that Wittgenstein here describes as a system of reference, it makes no sense to think that one can first establish the truth of that belief and then use it as a reason for adopting the system of reference. On the contrary, one could not acquire a belief in God's existence without both understanding and committing oneself to the broader grammatical system in which the concept of God has its life. (Mulhall, 2001: 101)

In other words, and as we have already seen, belief in God is not, for Wittgenstein, a purely intellectual hypothesis that one can understand and assess independently of understanding the role the concept of God plays in the religious practice and the life of the religious believer. The 'disagreement' between religious believer and non-believer is not, therefore, a 'normal controversy' that could be settled by appeal to the 'modern scientific criteria'. To think otherwise is just to reject Wittgenstein's whole conception out of hand and to insist that religious belief cannot be anything other than what Wittgenstein calls 'superstition' – pseudo-scientific or empirical belief that rests on very 'flimsy' evidence.

What is more, in the passage that Hyman singles out for criticism (CV 73/64), Wittgenstein is not saying that religious belief is 'nothing but' commitment to a system of reference; he says it is 'something like' commitment to such a system. So, it does not go without saying (as Hyman seems to assume) that such commitment is incompatible with believing that religious beliefs express truths – it merely rejects the idea that it makes sense to think that this can be done in a grammar-independent and context-invariant way (more on this in Section 4). Consequently, to say that religious belief is neither reasonable nor unreasonable is not to say that it is irrational, or indeed invulnerable to criticism.[43] It is only to reject a particular way of construing religious belief, namely, as a defective kind of empirical or meta-empirical belief.

Hyman also appears to overlook the fact that there is, in the end, no fundamental difference between commitment to a religious 'system of reference' and commitment to our ordinary 'epistemic system', since all systems ultimately

---

[43] For example, one could criticize Christianity in a Nietzschean manner as embodying not just self-hatred, but also the inability to face up to the radical contingency and meaninglessness of life. Or, as Mulhall points out, one could share Freud's suspicions that institutionalized religion panders to psychologically immature dependence on a father figure (Mulhall, 2001: 106), etc.

presuppose, as Pritchard points out, arational 'hinge' commitments (Pritchard, 2021, 2022). 'Hinge' or 'framework' commitments are those commitments that must stand fast (and that, consequently, cannot be doubted), even though no further justification of them is possible, as 'justification comes to an end' (*On Certainty* (OC) §192).

In his last collection of remarks, *On Certainty*, Wittgenstein puts it thus: 'That is to say, the *questions* that we raise and our *doubts* depend on the fact that some propositions are exempt from doubt, are as it were like hinges (*Angeln*) on which those turn' (OC §341). 'Those propositions that are exempt from doubt', and that provide the 'hinges' upon which the propositions that *can* be investigated turn, have come to be known, in the literature, as 'hinge-propositions'.[44] They are the propositions that must stand fast, if epistemic enquiry is to be possible at all, and which, therefore, play a 'fulcrum' role (Pritchard, 2022).

When Wittgenstein says, at CV 73/64, that religious belief could only be something like a passionate commitment to a system of reference, he uses the same turn of phrase that he also employs in OC to characterize our 'framework' or 'hinge' commitments: *Bezugssystem*, which in OC §83, for example, gets translated as 'frame of reference', whereas Winch, in CV, renders it as 'system of reference'. Since the German word is the same in both these texts, however, it seems reasonable to assume that what Wittgenstein means by it in CV is similar, if not identical, to what he means in OC.

So, if our epistemic practices in general – our epistemic *Bezugssystem* – presuppose arational hinge commitments that admit of no further justification (if you dig down deep enough), and religious commitment is also a commitment to a system of reference, then perhaps one of the things that Wittgenstein means when he says that religious belief is neither reasonable nor unreasonable is that this system also presupposes such arational hinge-commitments. What is more, if we are able to recognize that nothing is wrong with this in the epistemic case, but rather that it could not be otherwise,[45] then the conclusion to draw is that this is not to count as a defect in the religious case either.[46] Belief in God, for the person who has faith, is a religious hinge-commitment that cannot be justified by way of appeal to empirical (or 'metaphysical') evidence, as the concept of 'God' is not the name of a super-empirical entity whose existence is in doubt. This is why, and as Mulhall says, one could not acquire a belief in God 'without both understanding and committing

---

[44] See, for example, Williams (1996), Moyal-Sharrock (2004), Wright (2004a, 2004b), Coliva (2010, 2015), Pritchard (2014, 2015) and Schönbaumsfeld (2016a, 2016b, 2021).

[45] I cannot defend these insights here. For a defence, see Schönbaumsfeld (2016a, 2016b, 2021). For alternative proposals, see Williams (1996), Moyal-Sharrock (2004), Wright (2004a, 2004b), Coliva (2010, 2015), and Pritchard (2014, 2015).

[46] Compare Pritchard (2021, 2022).

oneself to the broader grammatical system in which the concept of God has its life' (Mulhall, 2001: 101). But, if this is right, then (1) and (2) are false.

Does any of this imply that Wittgenstein is espousing a form of fideism (or 'quasi-fideism', as Pritchard (2021, 2022)) contends,[47] either in epistemology or religion? No. What Wittgenstein is doing is clarifying the grammar of our practices by showing that it makes no sense to assume that our relation to our systems of reference is epistemic all the way down: 'I did not get my picture of the world by satisfying myself of its correctness; nor do I have it because I am satisfied of its correctness. No: it is the inherited background against which I distinguish between true and false' (OC §94). That is to say, just as a game, in order to be a game, must have rules distinct from the moves the rules make possible, so our practices also require an unquestioned background – something that stands fast – in order to function, and against which the specific moves can be assessed.[48]

Of course, committing to a religious 'system of reference' is 'optional' in the sense that if one were to lose one's faith, this would not constitute an annihilation of *all* yardsticks (OC §492) (an annihilation of all principles of judgement) in the way that doubting our most fundamental (non-religious) hinge-commitments would (such as, say, genuinely doubting that one had hands in ordinary circumstances). So, in this respect, there is a clear asymmetry between our most fundamental hinge-commitments and what one could call more 'personal' hinge-commitments (such as religious belief) that need not be shared by others. Nevertheless, what makes belief in God a 'hinge' is not that this belief must be shared by everyone, but that loss of faith is not the loss of a merely isolated intellectual belief: if I lose my faith in God, I don't just give up a single, independently specifiable, commitment, I lose a whole 'world' – the entire Christian 'system of reference', for example, in which my faith played its 'fulcrum' role.

It is also worth emphasizing that although hinge-commitments play the role of principles of judgement in the relevant form of life and are, in this much, the logical enabling conditions that allow the practice to operate, this does not imply that commitment to these principles, although epistemically groundless

---

[47] I agree with quite a few of the insights that Pritchard (2021, 2022) offers (although my conception of hinges is different from his – see Schönbaumsfeld, 2016b), but I don't think it's a good idea to call Wittgenstein's position 'fideistic' – be it 'quasi' or not. For not only would we otherwise have to conclude that Wittgenstein's position, in OC, is also 'quasi-fideistic' (given that Pritchard is importing some of OC's insights into the position he calls 'quasi-fideism'), the label further gives the impression that this is a 'faute de mieux' position: it would be much better to have known rational foundations, but we must rest content with faith or 'animal certainty'. Now, I'm sure that this is not what Pritchard, in fact, means, but critics of Wittgenstein have employed the word in this manner, so I don't think its use is felicitous. Regrettably, Pritchard also believes that Wittgenstein's view, in LC, is fideistic (Pritchard, 2021), and for the reasons given in this section, I believe this to be an incorrect assessment.

[48] For more on this, see Schönbaumsfeld (2016b).

in the sense that they admit of no further justification (since they themselves constitute what the 'base line' is), is, therefore, entirely reasonless or arbitrary. For, as we saw in Section 2, life can force the concept of God upon us – that is, one's personal experiences can give one reason to believe in God. But these reasons are not 'evidence' in the sense that they epistemically ground the belief such that any rational agent would be forced to adopt it.

An example from another context might help to make this point explicit. Scientists, for instance, prefer theories that are 'simple'. In this respect, 'simplicity' serves as a principle of judgement when it comes to adjudicating between competing theories. But the preference for simplicity is not itself evidentially grounded, for, in order to be able to assess the proposition 'simple theories are more truth-conducive than complex ones', the principles of judgement to be justified must always already be in place. In spite of this, adoption of the principle is not arbitrary: we might have aesthetic reasons for preferring simplicity, or we might already be committed to the notion that nature must be explainable by means of the smallest number of natural laws. As Wittgenstein says, 'Remember that one is sometimes convinced of the *correctness* of a view by its *simplicity* or *symmetry*, i.e., these are what induce one to go over to this point of view. One then simply says something like: "*That's* how it must be"' (OC §92).

If this is right, Wittgenstein is not endorsing the view that commitment to a system of reference – in religion or elsewhere – is a matter of arbitrary choice. Neither does he hold that faith itself 'epistemically grounds' religious belief (as the Reformed Epistemologists[49] contend, for example). So, Wittgenstein's position is not best characterized as fideistic. Rather, he rejects as confused the idea that religious belief involves isolated super-empirical beliefs that must be evidentially grounded in the manner of scientific hypotheses.

In Section 5, we will revisit some of this terrain when considering the question of whether Wittgenstein's conception leads to a form of relativism. But before we do that, we need to take a closer look at Wittgenstein's view of religious language.

4 Religious Language

4.1 Introduction

In the conversation with Rhees already mentioned in Sections 1 and 2, Wittgenstein says:

> Our statements about God have a different grammar from our statements about human beings. And if you try to talk about God as you would talk about

---

[49] See, for example, Plantinga (2000).

a human being, you are likely to come to talk nonsense, to ask nonsensical questions and so on. In talking about God we often use images or parts of images that apply to human beings. This is so when we say: 'Wherever you are, God always sees what you do.' We know how this statement is used, and that is all right.

So we may speak also of God's hearing our prayers. You might say then that in our picture of God there are eyes and ears. But it makes no sense if you then try to fill in the picture and think of God as having teeth and eyelashes and stomach and tendons and toenails. So we might say that our picture of God is like a picture of a human being with holes in it. Which means that the grammar of our language about God has holes in it if you look at it as the grammar of statements about a human being.

In describing our picture of God we may speak of it as being made up of parts of a picture of a human being together with other things which have no resemblance to any part of a human being. You might start the description of a curve by taking drawings of familiar curves: a circle, an ellipse, a parabola, a hyperbola. Then describe it by saying: 'You see here it is part of a parabola, there then it is part of a circle, here it is a straight line which goes into part of a spiral, etc.' And the curve you described might then have an equation entirely unlike any of the familiar curves.

(Rhees, 2001: 413)

What Wittgenstein appears to be saying in this passage is that the grammar of 'God' contains aspects of human grammar, such as talk of God 'hearing' and 'seeing', 'together with other things which have no resemblance to any part of a human being'. He then goes on to compare a description of this grammar to that of a very strange new curve, which also contains some familiar parts – for example, parabola-parts, circular parts, parts of a spiral – while nevertheless having an equation which is 'entirely unlike any of the familiar curves'. In the present section, I want to elucidate what Wittgenstein means by this analogy and what implications it has for an understanding of religious language. This will also enable us to respond to some widespread criticisms of Wittgenstein's view and bolster our argument against the contention that Wittgenstein is promoting a form of non-cognitivism.

4.2 'External' and 'Internal' Understanding

A common misconception about sentence-meaning consists in the idea that it is a mere aggregate of word-meaning: if I know what all the individual words in a sentence mean, I know what the sentence as a whole means. Let's call this an atomistic conception of sentence-meaning. Although Wittgenstein has no sympathy for this view in any domain of discourse, it is particularly disastrous for the attempt to understand the meaning of religious language. In order to see why, let's look at the following passage from Nielsen (Nielsen & Phillips, 2005):

> It is not [. . .] that I think that God is an object among objects, but I do think [. . .] that he must – in some very unclear sense – be taken to be a particular existent among existents though, of course, 'the king' among existents, and a very special and mysterious existent, but not an object, not a kind of object, not just a categorical or classificatory notion, but not a non-particular either. Though he is said to be infinite, he is also said to be a person, and these two elements when put together seem at least to yield a glaringly incoherent notion. He cannot be an object – a spatio-temporal entity but he is also a he – a funny kind of he to be sure – who is also said to be a person – again a funny kind of person – who is taken to be a person without a body: a purely *spiritual* being. This makes him out to be a 'peculiar reality' indeed. He gets to be even more peculiar when we are told he is an *infinite* person as well. But now language has really gone on a holiday. (Nielsen & Phillips, 2005: 123)

These remarks illustrate extremely well how the similarities and differences between the grammar of 'God' and descriptions of ordinary human beings can confound us. On the one hand, God is said to be a person, which appears to make God akin to a human being; on the other, God is described as 'infinite', and, hence, as radically different from a human person. Small wonder that Nielsen ends up concluding that what we have here is a glaringly incoherent notion.

The way out of the quandary consists in heeding Wittgenstein's warning that, despite containing some familiar parts (words), the 'equation' we are confronted with is 'entirely unlike any of the familiar curves'. Consequently, we need to be wary of supposing, as does Nielsen, that there is nothing more to understanding the sentence 'God is an infinite person' than combining the individual atoms, 'infinite' and 'person', into a peculiar complex. What is more, we can also not assume – and this is a further mistake that Nielsen makes – that it is possible to inspect the words alone in order to find out whether they make sense or not. For this is to ignore Wittgenstein's injunction that 'practice gives the words their sense': that we cannot find out what words mean without attending to the particular context of use in which these words have their life.

Hence, if we are to have any hope of understanding what it means to call God infinite, we must attend to the overall use to which this form of words is put in the religious practice as a whole. That is to say, we cannot assume that because we know what 'infinite' means in a non-religious context, we automatically know what it means to say that God is infinite. For the sentence is more than the sum-total of its individually meaningful parts, as Wittgenstein already realized in the *Tractatus*: 'Only propositions have sense; only in the nexus [*Zusammenhang*] of a proposition does a name have meaning' (3.3). In other words, the overall sense of the sentence contributes to the meaning of the individual parts (words). Consequently, sentence-meaning cannot be derived from a summation of the meanings of the individual parts (say, the meanings that a dictionary gives you). This implies that Nielsen is wrong to think that he should, straightforwardly, be able to understand discourse about God just because he is familiar with the individual words that the religious person uses to speak about God. For, as we have already seen in previous chapters, the grammar of 'God' – despite sharing features with ordinary descriptions of human beings – is really quite different from that of a human person (even a super-powerful one).

But Nielsen makes a further mistake, not unconnected to the previous ones: he assumes that the prime function of religious language is to convey information about God. It is doubtful, however, whether the religious believer wants to inform anyone of a state of affairs when he says, for example, that God is infinite. Rather, this form of words appears to function more like a profession of faith than a straightforward description.[50] Later Wittgenstein is good on the distinction between sentences having a merely instrumental use (where that use is primarily to convey information of some sort), and sentences being, as it were, ends in themselves:

> If we compare a proposition to a picture [as Wittgenstein did in the *Tractatus*], we must consider whether we are comparing it to a portrait (a historical representation) or to a genre-picture. And both comparisons make sense.
>
>   When I look at a genre-picture, it 'tells' me something, even though I don't believe (imagine) for a moment that the people I see in it really exist, or that there have really been people in that situation. For suppose I ask, '*What* does it tell me, then?' (PI §522)
>
> 'A picture tells me itself' is what I'd like to say. That is, its telling me something consists in its own structure, in *its* own form and colours. (PI §523)

In these passages, Wittgenstein seems to be identifying two ways in which a sentence can 'tell' me something: either by straightforwardly conveying information about a particular state of affairs – where this information could also be conveyed by some other means (or by using a different sentence that expresses the same thought) – or by 'telling me something' in a way that is not specifiable independently of using the precise form of words employed. In the first case, the thought expressed in the sentence could easily be paraphrased without loss; in the second case, the sentence in question could not easily be replaced by another which says the same. Wittgenstein clarifies:

---

[50] D. Z. Phillips was one of the first philosophers to make this clear. See, for example, Phillips (1965/2014).

> We speak of understanding a sentence in the sense in which it can be replaced by another which says the same; but also in the sense in which it cannot be replaced by any other. (Any more than one musical theme can be replaced by another.)

> In the one case, the thought in the sentence is what is common to different sentences; in the other, something that is expressed only by these words in these positions. (Understanding a poem.) (PI §531)

If the particular turn of phrase used is crucial to understanding, and in this respect not replaceable by another 'which says the same', then this implies that one's understanding of the relevant construction cannot be displayed merely by being able to paraphrase the form of words in question. Since it seems plausible that this insight does not just apply to poetry and music, but also to religious language-use, this means that Nielsen is rather rashly supposing that knowing what 'infinite' means, say, in a mathematical context, is easily going to be transposable into a religious context. 'Then has "understanding" two different meanings here?' asks Wittgenstein. No: 'I would rather say that these kinds of use of "understanding" make up its meaning, make up my *concept* of understanding. For I *want* to apply the word "understanding" to all this' (PI §532).

Following Wittgenstein's distinction, we can call the kind of understanding that consists only of being able to offer a passable paraphrase of the sentence in question 'external' understanding, whereas the kind of understanding that consists of being able to see that the form of words in question is not instrumentally intersubstitutable (not replaceable by another 'which says the same'), can be called 'internal' to register the fact that what is grasped in the sentence is 'internal' to this specific arrangement of words.[51] Applying this distinction to the passage from Nielsen, we can, therefore, say that Nielsen is missing the internal dimension of understanding when it comes to discourse about God. Nielsen possesses an 'external' understanding, in the sense that he knows what the relevant words mean in other contexts, and could, to this extent, offer a paraphrase of 'God is infinite', but he fails to see that these words might have a use that is not primarily informational or descriptive.

The fact that Nielsen fails to see this is connected to his assumption that the whole sentence is no more than the sum of its parts (the atomistic conception of sentence-meaning). For an internal understanding that consists in recognizing how this particular form of words cannot be replaced by another which says the same is antithetical to a conception that presupposes that sentence-meaning can be found through a process of 'aggregation'. So, to return to Wittgenstein's curve analogy, as long as one remains at the level of external understanding, all that one will see is that this strange curve seems to be a hodgepodge of

---

[51] This terminology is Ridley's (2004: 32–3). I first made use of it in Schönbaumsfeld (2007: 182–3).

incoherently put together parts: part parabola, part spiral and so forth. If, however, one recognizes that this curve has an equation quite different from all the familiar curves, then, instead of prioritizing what one believes are the familiar parts and attempting to aggregate them into a recalcitrant whole, one will start by focussing on the whole in order to see how it (the whole) transforms the significance of its parts. This means not focussing on the whole in isolation – as it were in a vacuum – but in the context of the entire practice in which this whole plays a role.

In other words, it is not possible to explain the meaning of religious language merely by attempting to paraphrase it; by trying to distil out its informational content, as it were. For this, to use Cottingham's picturesque expression, is to employ a 'fruit-juicer' method: to require 'the clear liquid of a few propositions to be extracted for examination in isolation from what [one] take[s] to be the irrelevant pulpy mush of context' (Cottingham, 2009: 209). And such a procedure, as Cottingham notes, does not give you the essence of a fruit, but only a not very palatable drink plus a pulpy mess.

Arguably, Frazer applies a very similar method when characterizing the religious practices of tribes as forms of false science. For Frazer, like Nielsen, seems to possess only an 'external' understanding of ritualistic activity that can see nothing in such practices but the attempt to influence the course of events by empirically inept means, when the point of such practices may be no such thing. In other words, the attempt to distil out the 'empirical content' of religious ritual – what the ritual attempts to 'achieve' – subjects it to severe distortion: 'It is nonsense to go on and say that the characteristic feature of these actions is that they spring from erroneous notions about the physics of things. (As Frazer does when he says that magic is really false physics, or as the case may be, false medicine, technology, etc.)' (RFGB §15). Rather, Wittgenstein suggests, we need to learn to see that 'when one observes the life and behaviour of humans all over the earth, one sees that apart from the kinds of behaviour one could call animal, the intake of food, etcetera, etcetera, etcetera, humans also carry out actions that bear a peculiar character, and might be called ritual actions' (RFGB §15). Ritual actions do not have an instrumental aim (as Frazer misguidedly believes), but are rather ends in themselves. Appreciation of the fact that humans are, as Wittgenstein says, 'ceremonial animals' (RFGB §15) is the first step towards an 'internal' understanding of religious rituals.

We can now apply these insights to making sense of Wittgenstein's conversation with Rhees. At the beginning of the conversation, Wittgenstein says, '"Wherever you are, God always sees what you do." We know how this statement is used, and that is all right' (Rhees, 2001: 413). Here Wittgenstein appears to think that we would not get into confusion about the use of this statement, perhaps because the phrase and its application are so familiar to us: we do not take it that God has strange Argus-eyes that are able to see all there is to be seen; rather, the sentence serves to remind us that God is always aware of what we are doing and judging our actions (even if we manage to hide them from others). Or, to use another religious expression, God is omnipresent.

In respect to the latter phrase, however, we could easily imagine how confusion might ensue – namely, if we were to model the grammar of 'God is omnipresent' on what it would be like for a human to be omnipresent; that is to say, simultaneously in all places at once. Naturally, if we construed the grammar thus, and hence offered a paraphrase of the sentence along such lines, then the statement would immediately strike us as incoherent and absurd, since it is necessarily impossible for an entity to be in all places at the same time.

Arguably, Nielsen is guilty of making the same mistake, as he also appears to model the grammar of God as 'infinite person' on human grammar. For God, on Nielsen's construction, is a type of *entity* that is describable as 'infinite' – without limits, endless or everlasting – an idea that is, indeed, hard to make sense of if we think of something 'bounded' and finite, such as a human person.[52] Had Nielsen proceeded more holistically, however, he might have realized that use of the word 'infinite' precisely signals that we cannot be speaking of something that one would ordinarily call an 'entity' at all. This is why Wittgenstein says, 'the way you use the word "God" does not show *whom* you mean, but what you mean' (CV 58/50). And this is not a profession of atheism on Wittgenstein's part, but a grammatical remark that is supposed to alert us to the fact that the grammar of 'God' does not function like the grammar of an entity or 'person' in the ordinary sense.

The upshot of all this is that it is only possible to develop an internal understanding of religious language-use if one attends to the depth grammar of the relevant expressions, instead of being mesmerized by superficial similarities between God-talk and discourse about ordinary, empirical things. That is to say, although 'in our picture of God there are eyes and ears', 'it makes no sense if you then try to fill in the picture and think of God as having teeth and eyelashes and stomach and tendons and toenails'.

In other words, when we speak of the 'eye' of God or of God 'hearing' our prayers, we are using these words in a different sense than in ordinary discourse where what we mean by 'eye' is a physical sense-organ and by 'hearing' we refer to a certain auditory process. Nonetheless, and as Wittgenstein makes clear in PPF, where he talks about calling particular days of the week 'fat' and 'lean',

---

[52] It's not much easier to make sense of the notion if we think, instead, of an abstract object.

it is precisely because the words have the ordinary meanings that they do, that we now want to employ them in this new way:

> Given the two concepts 'fat' and 'lean', would you be inclined to say that Wednesday was fat and Tuesday lean, or the other way round? (I am strongly inclined towards the former.) Now have 'fat' and 'lean' some different meaning here from their usual one? – They have a different use. – So ought I really to have used different words? Certainly not. – I want to use *these* words (with their familiar meanings) *here*. (PPF §274 ; xi: 216)

> Asked 'what do you really mean here by "fat" and "lean"?', I could only explain the meanings in the usual way. I could *not* point them out by using Tuesday and Wednesday as examples. (PPF §274 ; xi: 216)

> Here one might speak of a 'primary' and 'secondary' meaning of a word. Only someone for whom the word has the former meaning uses it in the latter.
> (PPF §274 ; xi: 216)

Something very interesting is going on in these passages. Despite often being (erroneously) labelled a use-theorist of meaning, Wittgenstein says that although 'fat' and 'lean' have a different *use* when applied to days of the week, he nevertheless hesitates to say that they have a different meaning. What is more, Wittgenstein emphasizes that he could only explain what 'lean' and 'fat' mean in this context in the ordinary way, which seems to imply that it is not possible to learn the new use merely by knowing what the words mean in ordinary contexts. Nonetheless, the new use is parasitic on the old use: only someone for whom the words have the old use will be inclined to use the words in this novel way.

So, is what Wittgenstein calls 'secondary sense' something like metaphorical meaning? Wittgenstein says 'no': 'If I say, "For me the vowel *e* is yellow", I do not mean 'yellow' in a metaphorical meaning – for I could not express what I want to say in any other way than by means of the concept of yellow' (PPF §274 ; xi: 216). While one could challenge the thought that it is always necessary for something's being a metaphor that whatever it is that the metaphor is saying could also be expressed in another way, one can take Wittgenstein's point that what is essential to secondary sense is that I want to employ *these* words in *these* positions (compare PI §531). One cannot easily replace these words with something else.

It seems natural to connect the employment of words in a secondary sense with what Diamond (2005) calls a 'conceptual reorientation'. Such a reorientation occurs in situations where I am moved to employ old concepts in novel ways. Diamond gives the example of suddenly finding it apt to call George Eliot 'beautiful', in despite of the fact that, according to conventional criteria of beauty, Eliot is not a beautiful woman:

> She [George Eliot], that magnificently ugly woman, gives a totally transformed meaning to 'beauty'. Beauty itself becomes something entirely new for one. As one comes to see (to one's own amazement, perhaps) a powerful beauty residing in this woman [. . .] In such a case, she is not judged by a norm available through the concept of beauty; she shows the concept up, she moves one to use the words 'beauty' and 'beautiful' almost as new words, or as renewed words. She gives one a new vocabulary, a new way of taking the world in in one's words and of speaking about it to others. (Diamond, 2005: 125)

In this example, Diamond seems to be suggesting, George Eliot herself provides a new criterion for employment of the concept 'beauty', rather than being judged by a norm made available through prior use of the concept. And something similar may happen in a religious context, when someone experiences a conversion and expresses this experience with the form of words: 'God is infinite' or 'God is omnipresent'.

Of course, there may be people who are unable to see how one could extend the concept of beauty to George Eliot, just as there are people who cannot see what it could mean to speak of God's infinitude. Not all potentially available secondary uses of concepts are equally available to everyone, just as certain aspects of the world can be perceived by some that others are impervious to. Fortunately, it is possible to work on oneself in order to make new forms of seeing and understanding possible. This is why Wittgenstein says:

> In religion it must be the case that corresponding to every level of devoutness there is a form of expression that has no sense at a lower level. For those still at the lower level this doctrine, which means something at the higher level, is null & void; it *can* only be understood *wrongly*, & so these words are *not* valid for such a person. (CV 37/32).

In other words, the same form of expression can do different work for different people. What sense someone can make of an expression will, therefore, depend on the relative level of spiritual development of the person concerned. For instance, someone who thinks that Job's words 'the Lord has given, the Lord has taken away, blessed be the name of the Lord' are a cheap attempt at trying to justify the malevolent arbitrariness of the deity, is at a lower level of religious understanding than someone who sees it as an expression of one's trusting acceptance of God's sovereignty. Similarly, someone who believes that 'God is infinite' is an incoherent metaphysical claim about a bizarre entity, possesses less religious insight than someone who recognizes that it is an expression that shows that, for the religious believer, God surpasses everything.

None of this is peculiar to the religious domain. In aesthetics, ethics and philosophy – in addition to music and other artistic endeavours – it is similarly true that one's understanding grows in proportion to how much one is able to develop certain relevant capacities: one's musicality, sensitivity, attention to detail, open-mindedness, altruism and so on. Why should it be any different in religion and the expectation be that whatever immediately meets the eye (or ear) must be sufficient to know what is meant? As we have already seen, the surface appearance may be extremely deceptive and embroil us in all sorts of confusions, if we are not vigilant.

Consequently, we must be careful that the familiar we recognize does not occlude the unfamiliar we need to make sense of. Otherwise, instead of realizing that we are confronted by 'an equation entirely unlike all familiar curves', we will rashly end up concluding that the grammar of God 'has holes in it', or, indeed, that it is, in Nielsen's words, 'plain incoherent'. Both responses can be avoided, if we look at the depth grammar and recognize that much religious discourse employs words in a secondary sense – a sense that can only be understood if we don't just inspect the words alone, but learn more about the religious practices in which these concepts have their life.

4.3 Non-cognitivism?

At this point in the discussion, an apparently hard-nosed reader might want to say something like this: 'If you are right that much religious language employs words in a secondary sense, is this not tantamount to saying that it is used only to express an attitude?'[53] In other words, is Wittgenstein not really propagating a non-cognitive conception of religious belief, according to which all that is required is a passionate commitment to a 'content-free', or 'doctrineless', form of life?

It should already be apparent from our previous discussion that there can be no such thing as 'grammar-free' doctrine for Wittgenstein. Consequently, what the Christian doctrine amounts to – and, hence, what is involved in believing it – cannot be determined by inspecting the words alone (outside of their specific context of use). But accepting this insight does not imply endorsing the notion that, therefore, there is no doctrine, just 'attitudes' (Wittgenstein is not Don Cupitt[54] in disguise). Rather, Wittgenstein is in the business of trying to elucidate precisely what the grammar of the doctrine involves and how it differs from the grammar of ordinary empirical descriptions, for example.

Furthermore, and as we have already seen in Section 2, Wittgenstein is not saying that religious belief is not *belief*. Instead, Wittgenstein is emphasizing that *although* it's belief, it's *also* a way of living (CV 73/64). That is to say, the

---

[53] See, for example, (Glock, 1995), (Hyman, 2001) and (Nielsen, 2005) for proponents of such an interpretation of Wittgenstein.

[54] See, for example, Cupitt (2003).

word 'belief' functions differently when applied to religious faith than it does in ordinary discourse. This should not surprise us. Since Wittgenstein rejects the 'fruit juicer' method of specifying the content of religious statements, it is impossible to factorize religious beliefs into two kinds of component: the putative 'informational' content and the expression of a 'doctrine-free' 'emotional attitude', for instance, as such a conception would be at odds with Wittgenstein's entire philosophy of language – it is not just due to the fact that Wittgenstein happens to hold an 'idiosyncratic' view about the nature of religious belief.

Neither does the use of words in a secondary sense have anything to do with the expression of an attitude, as opposed, say, to the endorsement of a 'cognitive' belief. If I say that the vowel 'e' is yellow or that the beginning of Wagner's 'Lohengrin overture' is blue, for example, I am not expressing an 'attitude' to the letter or the music – I am reporting how things strike me. Similarly, when the religious believer says that 'God is omnipresent', he is not expressing an attitude, but reporting his faith. This faith may, of course, engender various attitudes, such as an attitude of submission towards God, but the faith itself is not 'just' an attitude, if that means that it is a kind of 'content-free' feeling (which is usually what people who make this objection mean).

So, contrary to what Nielsen et al. believe, religious concepts and expressions are not, for Wittgenstein, the cognitively empty means to some practical end (say, leading a certain kind of life). Rather, the words and concepts used are as important as anything else. This is why Wittgenstein says, in LC, for instance, that the 'whole *weight* may be in the picture' (LC 72) that the religious person employs. That is to say, Wittgenstein's point is only that we cannot reach a mature understanding of what religious concepts (or pictures) involve independently of looking at the role they play in a religious believer's life. For this role will provide us with the clues to uncover the depth grammar of religious concepts. If we ignore this grammar, on the other hand, we will remain stuck at the level of surface grammar and never get beyond thinking that religion is a hodgepodge of strange metaphysical ideas, just as we may never be able to determine the equation of a new curve if we continue to cleave to the notion that it consists merely of familiar elements put together in an incoherent way.

Of course, many religious philosophers agree with Nielsen that the only way in which religious beliefs could be 'cognitive' and express truths is by being metaphysical claims, but, contrary to Nielsen, they regard this as perfectly coherent. In a response to Burley (2008), Haldane, for instance, makes this quite clear: 'If religious claims do not have metaphysical range, but are confined to the world of human imagination and commitment, then what is at issue is not the truth or falsity of naturalism but only the variety of its expressions'

(Haldane, 2008: 252). While I cannot here open the door to a discussion of naturalism (for more on how naturalism and religion can be compatible without one harming the other, see Ellis (2014)), the distinction that Haldane invokes strikes me as spurious, as it implies that if religious claims are not metaphysical ones, then they are merely figments of human imagination; that is, they cannot refer to anything real. This is like saying that if the language of mathematics does not have 'metaphysical range' – that is, is about a timeless realm of abstract objects – it is merely an imaginative construction. Both notions seem false and to presuppose commitment to Augustine's picture of language that we discussed, and dismissed, in Section 1. Far from being the final arbiter of what is to count as 'real' or 'human-independent', metaphysics, as Wittgenstein reminds us in RFGB, is itself a kind of magic – the confused attempt to conjure up entities in order to 'animate' our nouns and link them to a 'transcendent beyond'.

5 Incommensurability and Relativism

5.1 Introduction

If, as I have argued in previous sections, understanding religious language requires noticing new aspects in things, which, in turn, necessitates immersion in religious practice, then one might worry that atheists, or non-believers, are not able to understand religious discourse and are, consequently, unable to criticize it. Nielsen (Nielsen & Phillips, 2005) is particularly exercised by this potential implication of Wittgenstein's conception.[55] Kusch (2011), too, believes that some kind of incommensurability claim follows from the interpretation of Wittgenstein here proposed:

> 'Schönbaumsfeld hold[s] that for Wittgenstein religious language involves a "reorientation" of ordinary language. Moreover, [she] impl[ies] that the non-believer can come to grasp the meaning of religious language only by converting. And [she] suggest[s] that the non-believer suffers from a kind of conceptual aspect-blindness' (Kusch, 2011: 39).

While Kusch acknowledges that I reject the thought that religious discourse is 'incommensurable' with ordinary language, he remains unconvinced by my response that because religious language is parasitic on ordinary language-use, there cannot be a hard-and-fast divide between the former and the latter. Kusch's reasons for nevertheless remaining sceptical are as follows. First, he believes that the fact that religious discourse 'renews' ordinary words does not establish that this discourse is translatable into those words. Second, what – short of

---

[55] For a similar line of objection, see Law (2017).

a conversion – might enable the non-believer to understand these words? Third, grasping religious discourse for the first time seems to amount to a fundamental change in form of life, while understanding an artistic metaphor does not (Kusch, 2011: 40).

Kusch is right, of course, that it does not follow from religious discourse 'renewing' ordinary words that this discourse is translatable into those words. Indeed, if I am right that we need to understand religious expressions 'internally' (see Section 4), then such translation is precluded in virtue of the fact that what is essential to understanding religious phrases does not consist in the expressions' 'informational' content. So, it's true that religious language cannot straightforwardly be 'translated' into ordinary factual or empirical discourse. But no incommensurability claim follows from that. For, arguably, many forms of discourse are 'irreducible' (not incommensurable) in this way; aesthetic, ethical and even psychological language-uses springing immediately to mind. Many unsuccessful philosophical attempts have been made to 'translate' these forms of discourse into another – primarily into the 'language of science', perhaps[56] – but these scientistic tendencies should not be emulated.

Furthermore, and as we have already seen in Section 4, religious language cannot be 'incommensurable' with ordinary language, as without the habitual use of words, no 'renewed' religious use is possible, just as it is not possible to call Wednesday 'fat' unless one is able to make use of the ordinary way of employing the term. There is a parallel with aesthetic language-use here. Take the phrase 'Juliet is the sun'. If the word 'sun' did not mean the heavenly body, for example, then the construction 'Juliet is the sun' would lose its point. Nevertheless, it makes no sense to 'translate' the expression into 'Juliet is a hot heavenly body'. Similarly, the same applies to the phrase 'God's eye sees everything' (LC 71). If one didn't know the ordinary meaning of 'eye', then one wouldn't want to apply the word to God, just as one wouldn't want to say 'the vowel "e" is yellow' if one didn't know that 'yellow' means yellow. Nonetheless, one would badly miss the point if one thought that 'God's eye sees everything' can be paraphrased as 'the deity has a sense organ that can apprehend all there is to be seen', or if one thought that 'the vowel "e" is yellow' implied that vowels are yellow 'sense-data'.

None of this implies, though, that one actually has to *convert* in order to be able to learn the grammar of religious expressions. For example, one doesn't have to be a religious believer to understand that the depth grammar of the concept of God is not akin to that of a super-empirical object and that it consequently doesn't make sense to ask where God lives, or if he has tendons

---

[56] One need only think of Mackie's (1982) view of ethics or Churchland's (2013) attempt to reduce 'folk psychology' to the 'language' of neuroscience.

and toe-nails. So, transitions are fluid here: the basic grammar of religious expressions can be learnt by believers and unbelievers alike by attending closely to the religious form of life and the use to which religious expressions are put in it, but *some* aspects of religious doctrine and practice may remain closed to one if one is not a religious believer. This should not be surprising. Actual participants in a practice always have a different perspective from outsiders to the practice – it is one thing to *learn about* ballet technique, for instance, and quite another actually to be able to apply it. As we have already seen in Section 2, this is why Wittgenstein says that he could only utter the word 'Lord' with meaning if he lived completely differently.

Since it is possible to learn the grammar of religious expressions without converting, it is also possible (as we saw in Section 3) to criticize these practices.[57] Recall that one might think, like Nietzsche, for example, that a Christian conception of the self as inherently sinful and in need of redemption is inimical to human flourishing and hence to be avoided.[58] But that is probably not the kind of criticism that someone like Nielsen has in mind. What Nielsen wants to be able to say is that God-talk is incoherent tout court. Ironically, Wittgenstein would concur, if we take religious belief to be exhausted by the 'gaseous vertebrate' view: 'If this is religious belief, then it's all superstition' (LC 59). But Wittgenstein does not believe that this is all there is to it – people do not, he thinks, engage in religious practices out of sheer stupidity. And I suspect that's the real point of disagreement. People like Nielsen (or Mackie (1982), or Dawkins (2007)) want to be able to say that a purely 'external' understanding of religious language – which entails the 'gaseous vertebrate' view – is the only possible understanding: belief in God is either false or incoherent, and to see this requires no more than average intelligence. If I am right, however, there is a better way of understanding religious faith – Wittgenstein's 'third way' – which dexterously steers a course between the Scylla of a literalist cognitivism (the 'gaseous vertebrate' view') and the Charybdis of content-free commitments to a way of life (non-cognitivism).

In Sections 5.2 and 5.3, I will consider a further related problem: the question of whether Wittgenstein's conception leads to an objectionable form of relativism. To this end, I will begin with a critique of Kusch's interpretation of Wittgenstein as implying a 'relativism of distance' (Kusch, 2011: 42).

---

[57] For more on incommensurability, see Schönbaumsfeld (2007).

[58] One could also criticize religious practices on straightforwardly moral (not just ethical) grounds. For example, for being misogynistic, promoting anarchy, fostering divisiveness, inciting violence, etc. Whether such criticisms are justified depends on the religious practice in question and on what religious believers say and do. For an illuminating discussion of scripture and violence, see Snyder and Weiss (2020).

5.2 A Relativism of Distance?

Kusch believes that Wittgenstein would allow us to draw a distinction between what Kusch calls an 'ordinary' and an 'extraordinary' belief-attitude directed towards the *same* propositional content: 'Ordinary belief-attitudes are found in empirical and scientific beliefs; extraordinary belief-attitudes are characteristic of religious beliefs. [LC allows] that one and the same proposition – for instance, *that there will be a Last Judgement* – can serve as a propositional content for both an extraordinary and for an ordinary belief-attitude' (Kusch, 2011: 37). For instance, the person holding an 'ordinary' belief that God exists takes the same attitude towards the belief's propositional content as he would towards an ordinary empirical prediction – that is, he will regard it as more or less probable or as more or less well-supported by evidence – whereas the person holding an 'extraordinary' belief that God exists has a completely different, entirely 'firm', attitude not grounded in empirical evidence at all (Kusch, 2011: 38, 2012: 12).

It's hard to see how such a reading of Wittgenstein can be correct. For not only does Kusch's interpretation require us to adopt the 'factorization model', according to which the content of the religious belief can be divorced from the attitude taken towards it, the view also presupposes that Wittgenstein believes that this content can be specified in completely 'neutral' terms, and this must be false (see Sections 2 and 3). If, for example, I am Father O'Hara, and take an 'ordinary' belief-attitude towards the proposition that God exists because I believe that scientific evidence for God's existence is available, then this will have significant implications for what 'God exists' means. For, as we have seen in Section 3, 'making it a question of science' implies the gaseous vertebrate view, which Wittgenstein takes to be a misguided way of conceiving of God. Consequently, it cannot be the case that Father O'Hara and Wittgenstein's religious believer believe the same things (i.e. the same propositional content), since Father O'Hara believes that 'God' denotes a superpowerful entity for which there can be scientific evidence, whereas Wittgenstein's religious believer thinks that this constitutes a grammatical confusion. Hence, even if O'Hara's and Wittgenstein's religious believers employ the same word, 'God', to describe their beliefs, they cannot mean the same by their words. But, if so, the difference between them is not merely a difference in *attitude* but, simultaneously, also a difference in content.

We already saw in Section 2 that no clear distinction can be drawn, on my reading of Wittgenstein's conception, between 'living a certain way' and 'believing certain things', as ethical and religious beliefs can never be divorced from, and understood completely independently of, the difference they make in one's life. This is why Wittgenstein would reject the notion that religious beliefs are composed of two independent 'factors' – the belief's content and the belief-attitude. Rather, for Wittgenstein, form (attitude) and content are one.

This reinforces the point, contra Hyman and Nielsen, that Wittgenstein cannot be a non-cognitivist who seeks to reduce the content of religious beliefs to the expression of emotional attitudes, for if one cannot 'factor out' the attitude from the content, neither can one reduce one to the other. When Wittgenstein, therefore, says that 'Christianity is not a doctrine, not, I mean, a theory about what has happened and will happen to the human soul, but a description of something that actually takes place in human life' (CV 32/28), he does not mean that Christianity has no cognitive content. Neither is he implying that you can commit to the Christian form of life without, at the same time, committing yourself to the Christian claims. What he *is* denying is that any sense can be made of what it means to believe these claims independently of paying attention to the practices that give our words their sense (i.e. their grammar).

The foregoing has direct implications for whether any form of relativism follows from Wittgenstein's account. Relativism is the view that two people can form opposite beliefs on the basis of the same evidence and both be 'right'. It ought to be clear that on my reading of Wittgenstein, his conception is not relativistic in this sense. If believer and non-believer do not, necessarily, acquiesce to, or dissent from, the same propositional contents, then whatever the disagreement between them amounts to, it is not easily characterizable as a standard contradiction or, as we have seen, a 'normal controversy' (i.e. as affirming what the other person denies).

On Kusch's conception, too, Wittgenstein is not contradicting the religious believer, but for completely different reasons: while the religious believer has an 'extraordinary' belief-attitude to the proposition that there will be a Last Judgement, for example, Wittgenstein merely has the 'ordinary', 'empirical' belief-attitude towards there not being such a thing. Since these belief-attitudes are distinct, there is no conflict between what the two parties say. The reason why Kusch is nevertheless happy to speak of an 'extraordinary' disagreement in this case is that, even though the two parties do not straightforwardly contradict each other (since they have different belief-attitudes), they do 'disagree' about the *content* of their beliefs (since one of them believes that there will be a Last Judgement, while the other doesn't). Kusch, therefore, attributes a 'relativism of distance' (Kusch, 2011: 52) to Wittgenstein. A 'relativism of distance' implies that 'disagreements' between people who hold extraordinary beliefs and those that do not can be 'faultless'. I agree that there can be 'faultless *difference*' between religious believers and those who lack religious attitudes, but I think it is misleading to call this a form of relativism.

The reason why I would prefer to speak of 'faultless difference' rather than 'faultless disagreement' is, of course, that, contrary to Kusch, I do not think that the content of 'ordinary' and 'extraordinary' beliefs is the same. Consequently, believer and non-believer do not have a 'normal controversy':

> 'Suppose that someone believed in the Last Judgement, and I don't, does this mean that I believe the opposite to him, just that there won't be such a thing? I would say: "not at all, or not always" [...] "Do you contradict the man?" I'd say: "No"' (LC 53).

This passage seems directly to contradict Kusch's contention that Wittgenstein and the religious believer disagree in propositional content affirmed. So, it does not appear to be the case that Wittgenstein would endorse a relativism of distance that says that while believer and non-believer contradict each other in respect to the content of their beliefs, they can nevertheless both be 'right' in the sense that both an 'ordinary' and an 'extraordinary' belief-attitude can faultlessly be held.

There is also a problem with the notion of 'extraordinary evidence' that Kusch makes use of (Kusch, 2012: 14). For if 'extraordinary beliefs' have exactly the same content as ordinary empirical beliefs but are held on the basis of what seems to be, as Wittgenstein says, 'flimsy' evidence, why should we grant them any epistemic credibility at all? The reason why Kusch believes that 'ordinary' evidence is not evidence against 'extraordinary' belief is the following:

> Wittgenstein is adamant that one does not develop an attitude of extraordinary belief in response to mere ordinary evidence. Instead, it is the course of one's life as a whole that either causes one to have extraordinary beliefs or causes one not to have them. This cause is not a 'brute cause': it does not bring about extraordinary belief in the way a hit over the head or a drug might bring about a headache. It is a cause in terms of which the religious believer is able to make sense of his extraordinary beliefs, at least partially. And hence it seems appropriate to speak of this cause as 'extraordinary evidence'. (Kusch, 2012: 13–14)

I agree with Kusch that Wittgenstein is adamant that one does not develop a religious belief in response to mere 'ordinary evidence', but I'm not sure it is appropriate to speak instead of 'extraordinary evidence'. As we saw in Section 2, Wittgenstein believes that 'life' can educate one to a belief in God or 'force' this concept upon one (CV 97), but it does not follow from this that it therefore makes sense to say that 'life' provides one with 'extraordinary evidence' for the existence of God. For how, one might wonder, can life, taken as a whole, provide *evidence* for anything? One might just as well say that life provides one with 'extraordinary evidence' for animism, witches or the truth of scientology. And if, furthermore, animists, witch-worshippers and scientologists can 'faultlessly' disagree, then one would have, not a 'relativism of distance', but *rampant* relativism.

Kusch himself admits (in an email exchange) that one cannot take an extraordinary belief-attitude to just anything – for instance, to Wayne Rooney's being a fool (Kusch's example). But, if so, then some criteria are needed that would allow one to draw a line here, and it is hard to see where they might plausibly come from. What is more, it seems that such criteria would have to be driven by the *content* of what is believed, and this appears to be in tension with Kusch's contention that one can take both an 'ordinary' and an 'extraordinary' attitude to the same propositional content. For if certain contents are, as it were, more 'extraordinary attitude-apt' than others – which they would have to be if one wants to rule out that one can take an extraordinary attitude to 'just anything' – then all sorts of 'new' forms of 'unreasonable' belief will become possible. For example, one can take up an 'ordinary' attitude to something that is, in itself, an 'extraordinary' proposition, or take an 'extraordinary' attitude to something that 'really' only has empirical content. It is difficult to see either how one could make sense of such 'errors' or what it might mean to ascribe an 'intrinsic' content to a proposition, for the latter is clearly inconsistent with Wittgenstein's idea that meaning is use and therefore context-dependent.

For these reasons, the better option is to read Wittgenstein as rejecting altogether the notion that faith rests on an evidential basis. As we saw in Section 3, belief in God is something like passionate commitment to a system of reference, not to a super-empirical hypothesis for which 'scientific' evidence might become available. That is to say, one's life experiences may indeed give one reason to believe in God, but those reasons are not *evidence* – not even 'extraordinary' evidence – for God's existence, since 'evidence' ought to be something that everyone can independently appeal to as a justification, and this is simply not possible in the religious case. For, in respect of religion, one's reasons – to borrow a phrase from Moser – are 'volitionally sensitive' (Moser, 2013: 58): how one relates to one's life-experiences is itself not independent of one's overall sensibility and way of seeing things (one's *Weltanschauung*). Consequently, the overall shape of one's life or experiences may give one personal reasons to believe in God,[59] but it is misleading to call these reasons a form of 'evidence'. As Wittgenstein says:

> 'Unshakable faith. (E.g. in a promise.) Is it less certain than being convinced of a mathematical truth? – (But does that make the language games any more alike!)' (CV 84/73).

---

[59] See, in this respect, an interesting discussion of religious conversion in LePoidevin (2021).

Analogously, one might say: it is possible to employ the phrase 'extraordinary' evidence in the religious context, but that does little to make it any more similar to what one ordinarily calls 'evidence'. The language-games are very different here.

5.3 A Hinge-Commitment

If what I have argued in Section 5.2 is correct, Wittgenstein is not a relativist. There can be 'faultless difference' between the religious believer and the non-believer, in the sense that they each have different *Weltanschauungen*, but this, by itself, does not imply a form of relativism. For it is not the case that Wittgenstein thinks that believer and non-believer affirm or deny the same propositional contents while, at the same time, both being 'right' (i.e. having faultlessly held convictions). Indeed, it is questionable whether believer and non-believer are even 'on the same plane' (LC 56).

That they are not on the same plane seems to constitute one reason why arguments for the existence of God appear question-begging to the non-believer. For example, design arguments seem inconclusive, because one can only see divine governance in nature or the universe, if one already believes in divine governance. Given that there is no such thing as a self-validating experience or a self-interpreting rule, how one perceives certain events (or empirical facts) will itself already be shaped by one's world-picture. Consequently, if one doesn't already see nature in a certain way, namely, say, as something 'created' or 'sacred', one will not be persuaded by the thought that the beauty and complexity of the universe must presuppose a divine creator.

It is precisely for these reasons that it makes sense to regard belief in God as a hinge-commitment: it is the fulcrum of the religious believer's life, but there is no such thing as demonstrating – from 'neutral' grounds that everyone would agree to – that there is a God. The important thing to realize here is that this is not a shortcoming; rather, it couldn't be otherwise. If one could amass 'evidence' for God's existence, God would be a gaseous vertebrate – a super-empirical object – whose existence one could try to infer from 'footprints' or the movement of planets, for instance. Since Wittgenstein regards such a notion as confused, however, he also takes it as implausible to suppose that religious believers really come to have faith via demonstration or proof. Instead, Wittgenstein believes, such methods are only employed to give faith an intellectual foundation post hoc:

> A proof of God ought really to be something by means of which you can
> convince yourself of God's existence. But I think that *believers* who offered
> such proofs wanted to analyse & make a case for their 'belief' with their

intellect, although they themselves would never have arrived at belief by way of such proofs. 'Convincing someone of God's existence' is something you might do by means of a certain upbringing, shaping his life in such & such a way. (CV 97/85)

In other words, not proof, but a certain kind of education, is needed. Hinge-commitments aren't inculcated by adopting a new belief for which there is already a place in a system; rather, the 'system' itself must first be acquired. In this respect, religion and ethics are closely related: both faith and moral conscience are developed, not by means of an accumulation of 'evidence', but through painstaking work on oneself and one's way of seeing things (CV 24/16).

None of this implies, however, that one cannot engage in meaningful moral or religious debate with people who have different conceptions. One can try to convert a person who thinks differently to one's own point of view, and will, during this process, certainly give them reasons (not evidence). Nevertheless, just as rational argument alone will not suffice to convince the amoralist, neither will appealing to the 'wonder' of the universe suffice to convert the atheist. Rather, and as Wittgenstein says:

> Instruction in a religious faith, therefore, would have to take the form of a portrayal, a description, of that system of reference [*Bezugssystem*], while at the same time being an appeal to conscience.[60] And these together would have to result finally in the one under instruction himself, of his own accord, passionately taking up that system of reference. It would be as though someone were on the one hand to let me see my hopeless situation, on the other depict the rescue-anchor, until of my own accord, or at any rate not led by the hand by the *instructor*, I were to rush up & seize it. (CV 73/64)

Of course, one may not want to see the 'hopelessness of one's situation' or come to the conclusion that the 'means of rescue' is a fantasy. Wittgenstein himself struggled throughout his life to acquire faith and never felt that he had really managed to get there. But he took this to constitute a moral problem, not an 'opinion' arrived at for lack of evidence: 'I cannot kneel to pray, because it's as though my knees were stiff. I am afraid of dissolution (of my own dissolution) should I become soft' (CV 63/56). In other words, Wittgenstein fears that his ego would disintegrate in the dying to the self that religious belief seems to require.

6 Conclusion

If what I have argued in this Element is right, Wittgenstein's conception of religious belief can be defended against all the standard objections. Contrary to

---

[60] I have retained the 1977 translation here, as it seems superior to the later 'instructing in religious belief' for 'Instruktion in einem religiösen Glauben'.

what many philosophers and commentators believe, it is not the case that Wittgenstein's view is non-cognitivist, fideistic or implies an objectionable form of relativism. Rather, Wittgenstein presents us with an interesting and nuanced depiction of what religious belief involves and how it differs from ordinary empirical (or super-empirical) beliefs.

In order fully to appreciate Wittgenstein's conception, however, it is necessary to think outside the philosophical box and the standard dichotomies. As long as we continue to believe that there are only two ways of regarding matters – either religious beliefs are 'cognitive' and hence assimilable to ordinary empirical (or super-empirical/metaphysical) beliefs, or they are merely 'non-cognitive' expressions of attitudes and commitments to live a certain way – we will make no progress. On the reading I have been proposing, on the other hand, there is no such thing as dividing religious belief into two components: putative cognitive content and attitude taken towards the content. Rather, and as we have seen throughout this Element, for Wittgenstein, form and content are one: the 'how' of religious faith impacts the 'what' and vice versa – therefore, the two cannot be prised apart and assessed independently.[61]

Neither should we allow an overly narrow construction of 'realism' – be that in the theological domain, where it takes the form of excluding anything non-metaphysical or non-supernatural from 'religious reality', or in the secular one, where it takes the form of excluding anything non-empirical or 'non-natural' (often, two sides of the same coin) – to mislead us into writing off Wittgenstein's view as implying a 'religion for atheists'. Nothing Wittgenstein says entails that religious claims cannot be 'about anything real'. Rather, this remark itself stands in need of grammatical clarification. That is to say, we should not think that the word 'real' is itself context-invariant and that what it means to speak of different things being 'real' can always be settled in advance, and without paying attention to the particular context of use. For example, we speak of 'real inflation', 'real love', a 'real Leonardo', etc., but there isn't one common and invariant set of criteria that will cover all these different uses (or any new ones that might arise). Hence, what counts as 'real inflation' will be different from what we mean when we speak of a 'real Leonardo' or 'real love', etc.

So, we need to be careful that we don't impose an alien, or dogmatic, conception of 'reality' on practices where the grammar is different. For, if we do this in the religious case, we will end up with an O'Hara-type view that turns religion into a form of false science (superstition). On Wittgenstein's alternative

---

[61] The 'how' and the 'what' are notions that Kierkegaard's Climacus employs – the thought is mine.

construction, on the other hand, a much richer and more plausible interpretation of religious belief is available that doesn't reduce the grammar of God to that of a gaseous vertebrate. For, as Wittgenstein once said to Drury, 'If I thought of God as another being like myself, outside myself, only infinitely more powerful, then I would regard it as my duty to defy him' (Drury, 1981: 108).

Abbreviations

Works by Wittgenstein

CL	*Cambridge Lectures*
CV	*Culture and Value*
LC	*Lectures and Conversations on Aesthetics, Psychology and Religious Belief*
OC	*On Certainty*
PI	*Philosophical Investigations*
PPF	*Philosophy of Psychology, a Fragment* (formerly part II of PI)
RFGB	*Remarks on Frazer's* Golden Bough
TLP	*Tractatus Logico-Philosophicus*

Works by Kierkegaard

BA	*The Book on Adler*
CUP	*Concluding Unscientific Postscript to* Philosophical Fragments

References

Amesbury, R. (2022). Fideism. *The Stanford Encyclopaedia of Philosophy* (Summer 2022 Edition), E. N. Zalta (ed.). https://plato.stanford.edu/archives/sum2022/entries/fideism.

Andrejc, G. and Weiss, D., eds. (2019). *Interpreting Interreligious Relations with Wittgenstein: Philosophy, Theology and Religious Studies*. Leiden: Brill.

Asad, T. (2020). Thinking about Religion through Wittgenstein. *Critical Times* 3 (3), 403–42.

Barrett, C. (1991). *Wittgenstein on Ethics and Religious Belief*. Oxford: Blackwell.

Barth, K. (2003). *Church Dogmatics* vol. 1. G. W. Bromiley and T. F. Torrance (eds.). London and New York: T&T Clark.

Borowitz, E. (2006). *The Talmud's Theological Language-Game*. New York: SUNY Press.

Burley, M. (2008). Phillips and Eternal Life: A Response to Haldane. *Philosophical Investigations* 31 (3), 237–51.

Burley, M. (2012). Wittgenstein, Religion and the Rejection of Metaphysics. Conference contribution. https://bit.ly/3ElAccb.

Burley, M. (2018). Wittgenstein and the Study of Religion: Beyond Fideism and Atheism. In M. Burley (ed.), *Wittgenstein, Religion and Ethics: New Perspectives from Philosophy and Theology*. London: Bloomsbury, 49–76.

Churchland, P. (2013). *Matter and Consciousness*, 3rd ed. Harvard: MIT Press.

Clack, B. (1996). Wittgenstein and Expressive Theories of Religion. *International Journal for Philosophy of Religion* 40 (1), 47–61.

Clack, B. (1999). *An Introduction to Wittgenstein's Philosophy of Religion*. Edinburgh: Edinburgh University Press.

Coliva, A. (2010). *Moore and Wittgenstein: Scepticism, Certainty, and Common Sense*. Basingstoke: Macmillan.

Coliva, A. (2015). *Extended Rationality: A Hinge Epistemology*. London: Palgrave Macmillan.

Cottingham, J. (2009). Wittgenstein, Religion and Analytic Philosophy. In H.-J. Glock and J. Hyman (eds.), *Wittgenstein and Analytic Philosophy*. Oxford: Oxford University Press, 203–27.

Cupitt, D. (2003). *The Sea of Faith*, new ed. London: SCM Press.

Dawkins, R. (2007). *The God Delusion*. London: Penguin.

Diamond, C. (2005). Wittgenstein on Religious Belief: The Gulfs Between Us. In D. Z. Phillips and M. von der Ruhr (eds.), *Religion and Wittgenstein's Legacy*. Aldershot: Ashgate, 99–138.

Drury, M. O'C. (1981). Some Notes on Conversations with Wittgenstein. In R. Rhees (ed.), *Recollections of Wittgenstein*. Oxford: Oxford University Press.

Ellis, F. (2014). *God, Value, and Nature*. Oxford: Oxford University Press.

Glock, H.-J. (1995). *A Wittgenstein Dictionary*. Oxford: Blackwell.

Graham, G. (2014). *Wittgenstein and Natural Religion*. Oxford: Oxford University Press.

Haldane, J. (2007). Philosophy, Death and Immortality. *Philosophical Investigations* 30 (3), 245–65.

Haldane, J. (2008). Phillips and Eternal Life: A Response to Mikel Burley. *Philosophical Investigations* 31 (3), 252–60.

Holmer, P. (2012). *Selected Essays*. L. Barrett and D. Gouwens (eds.). Cambridge: The Lutterworth Press.

Hyman, J. (2001). The Gospel according to Wittgenstein. In M. Addis and R. L. Arrington (eds.), *Wittgenstein and Philosophy of Religion*. London: Routledge, 1–11.

Kerr, F. (1986). *Theology after Wittgenstein*. Oxford: SPCK Press.

Kierkegaard, S. (1980). *Sickness unto Death*. H. Hong and E. Hong (eds. and trans.). Princeton: Princeton University Press.

Kierkegaard, S. (1985). *Philosophical Fragments*. H. Hong and E. Hong (eds. and trans.). Princeton: Princeton University Press.

Kierkegaard, S. (1991). *Practice in Christianity*. H. Hong and E. Hong (eds. and trans.). Princeton: Princeton University Press.

Kierkegaard, S. (1992). *Concluding Unscientific Postscript to* Philosophical Fragments. H. Hong and E. Hong (eds. and trans.). Princeton: Princeton University Press.

Kierkegaard, S. (1998). *The Book on Adler*. H. Hong and E. Hong (eds. and trans.). Princeton: Princeton University Press.

Kusch, M. (2011). Disagreement and Picture in Wittgenstein's *Lectures on Religious Belief*. In R. Heinrich, E. Nemeth, W. Pichler and David Wagner. (eds.), *Image and Imaging in Philosophy, Science and the Arts*. Frankfurt am Main: Ontos, 35–57.

Kusch, M. (2012). Wittgenstein and the Epistemology of Peer Disagreement. https://bit.ly/3V5s5WV.

Law, S. (2017). Wittgensteinian Accounts of Religious Belief: Non-Cognitivist, Juicer, and Atheist-Minus. *European Journal of Philosophy* 25 (4), 1186–207.

LePoidevin, R. (2021). Religious Conversion and Loss of Faith: Cases of Personal Paradigm Shift? *Sophia* 60 (3), 551–66.

McCutcheon, F. (2001). *Religion within the Limits of Language Alone: Wittgenstein on Philosophy and Religion.* London: Ashgate.

Mackie, J. L. (1982). *The Miracle of Theism.* Oxford: Oxford University Press.

Malcolm, N. (1993). *Wittgenstein: A Religious Point of View?* New York: Cornell University Press.

Malcolm, N. (2001). *Ludwig Wittgenstein: A Memoir.* Oxford: Oxford University Press.

Monk, R. (1991). *The Duty of Genius.* London: Vintage.

Moore, A. (2003). *Realism and Christian Faith: God, Grammar, and Meaning.* Cambridge: Cambridge University Press.

Moser, P. K. (2013). God and Evidence: A Cooperative Approach. *European Journal for Philosophy of Religion* 5 (2), 47–61.

Moyal-Sharrock, D. (2004). *Understanding Wittgenstein's* On Certainty. London: Macmillan.

Mulhall, S. (2001). Wittgenstein and the Philosophy of Religion. In D. Z. Phillips and T. Tessin (eds.), *Philosophy of Religion in the 21st Century.* New York: Palgrave, 95–118.

Nielsen, K. and Phillips, D. Z. (2005). *Wittgensteinian Fideism?* London: SCM Press.

Phillips, D. Z. (1988). *Faith after Foundationalism.* London: Routledge.

Phillips, D. Z. (1993). *Wittgenstein and Religion.* London: Macmillan.

Phillips, D. Z. (2014). *The Concept of Prayer.* London: Routledge.

Plantinga, A. (2000). Religious Belief as Properly Basic. In B. Davies (ed.), *Philosophy of Religion: A Guide and Anthology.* Oxford: Oxford University Press, 42–94.

Pritchard, D. (2014). Entitlement and the Groundlessness of our Believing. In D. Dodd and E. Zardini (eds.), *Scepticism and Perceptual Justification.* Oxford: Oxford University Press, 190–212.

Pritchard, D. (2015). *Epistemic Angst.* Princeton: Princeton University Press.

Pritchard, D. (2021). Sceptical Fideism and Quasi-Fideism. *Manuscrito*, 44 (4), 1–21.

Pritchard, D. (2022). Exploring Quasi-Fideism. In D. Moyal-Sharrock and C. Sandis (eds.), *Extending Hinge Epistemology.* London: Anthem.

Putnam, H. (1992). *Renewing Philosophy.* Cambridge, MA: Harvard University Press.

Rhees, R. (1984). *Recollections of Wittgenstein.* Oxford: Oxford University Press.

Rhees, R. (2001). On Religion: Notes on Four Conversations with Wittgenstein. *Faith and Philosophy* 18 (4), 409–15.

Ridley, A. (2004). *The Philosophy of Music: Theme and Variation*. Edinburgh: Edinburgh University Press.

Schönbaumsfeld, G. (2007). *A Confusion of the Spheres: Kierkegaard and Wittgenstein on Philosophy and Religion*. Oxford: Oxford University Press.

Schönbaumsfeld, G. (2013). Kierkegaard and the *Tractatus*. In P. Sullivan and M. Potter (eds.), *Wittgenstein's* Tractatus*: History and Interpretation*. Oxford: Oxford University Press, 59–75.

Schönbaumsfeld, G. (2014). Wittgenstein and the 'Factorization Model' of Religious Belief. *European Journal for the Philosophy of Religion* 6 (1), 93–110.

Schönbaumsfeld, G. (2016a). 'Hinge Propositions' and the 'Logical' Exclusion of Doubt. *International Journal for the Study of Skepticism* 6 (2–3), 165–81.

Schönbaumsfeld, G. (2016b). *The Illusion of Doubt*. Oxford: Oxford University Press.

Schönbaumsfeld, G. (2018a). 'Meaning-Dawning' in Wittgenstein's *Notebooks*: A Kierkegaardian Reading and Critique. *British Journal for the History of Philosophy* 26 (3), 540–56.

Schönbaumsfeld, G. (2018b). On the Very Idea of a Theodicy. In M. Burley (ed.), *Wittgenstein, Religion and Ethics: New Perspectives from Philosophy and Theology*. London: Bloomsbury, 93–112.

Schönbaumsfeld, G. (2021). 'Logical' and 'Epistemic' Uses of 'to Know' or 'Hinges' as Logical Enabling Conditions. In C. Kyriacou and K. Wallbridge (eds.), *Sceptical Invariantism Reconsidered*. London: Routledge, 235–52.

Schönbaumsfeld, G. (in press). An Equation Entirely Unlike Any of the Familiar Curves: Wittgenstein on the Grammar of God and the Meaning of Religious Language. In M. Sievers and F. Suleiman (eds.), *The Grammar of God: Jewish, Christian and Islamic Perspectives*. Berlin: DeGruyter.

Schröder, S. (2007). The Tightrope Walker. *Ratio* 20 (4), 442–64.

Sievers, M. and Suleiman, F. (eds.) (in press). *The Grammar of God: Jewish, Christian and Islamic Perspectives*. Berlin: DeGruyter.

Snyder, J. and Weiss, D. (eds.) (2020). *Scripture and Religious Violence*. London: Routledge.

Swinburne, R. (2001). Philosophical Theism. In D. Z. Phillips and T. Tessin (eds.), *Philosophy of Religion in the 21st Century*. New York: Palgrave, 3–20.

Swinburne, R. (2016). *The Coherence of Theism*, 2nd ed. Oxford: Oxford University Press.

Williams, M. (1996). *Unnatural Doubts*. Princeton: Princeton University Press.

Williams, R. (2014). *The Edge of Words: God and the Habits of Language.* London: Bloomsbury.

Winch, P. (1987). *Trying to Make Sense.* Oxford: Blackwell.

Winch, P. (1995). *The Idea of a Social Science and its Relation to Philosophy.* London: Routledge.

Wittgenstein, L. (1922). *Tractatus Logico-Philosophicus.* C. K. Ogden (trans.). London: Routledge and Kegan Paul.

Wittgenstein, L. (2004). *Tractatus Logico-Philosophicus.* trans. B. F. McGuinness and D. F. Pears. London and New York: Routledge.

Wittgenstein, L. (1966). *Lectures and Conversations on Aesthetics, Psychology and Religious Belief.* C. Barrett (ed.). Oxford: Blackwell.

Wittgenstein, L. (1969). *On Certainty.* G. E. M. Anscombe and G. H. von Wright (eds.), G. E. M. Anscombe and D. Paul (trans.). Oxford: Blackwell.

Wittgenstein, L. (1977). *Culture and Value.* G. H. von Wright (ed.), P. Winch (trans.). Oxford: Blackwell.

Wittgenstein, L. (1998). *Culture and Value*, revised edition. G. H. von Wright (ed.), P. Winch (trans.). Oxford: Blackwell.

Wittgenstein, L. (1984). *Notebooks 1914–16*, 2nd ed. G. H. von Wright and G. E. M. Anscombe (eds.), G. E. M. Anscombe (trans.). Chicago: The University of Chicago Press.

Wittgenstein, L. (2009). *Philosophical Investigations*, 4th ed. P. M. S. Hacker and J. Schulte (ed.), G. E. M. Anscombe, P. M. S. Hacker and J. Schulte (trans.). Oxford: Blackwell.

Wittgenstein, L. (2016). *Lectures. Cambridge 1930–33.* D. G. Stern, B. Rogers and G. Citron (eds.). New York: Cambridge University Press.

Wittgenstein, L. (2018). *Remarks on Frazer's* Golden Bough. G. da Col and. S. Palmié (eds.), S. Palmié (trans.). Chicago: Hau Books.

Wright, C. (2004a). On Epistemic Entitlement: Warrant for Nothing (and Foundations for Free)? *Aristotelian Society Supplementary Volume* 78 (1), 167–212.

Wright, C. (2004b). Wittgensteinian Certainties. In Denis McManus (ed.), *Wittgenstein and Scepticism.* London: Routledge, 22–55.

Acknowledgements

I would like to thank Aaron Ridley, two anonymous referees, and David Stern for helpful comments on an earlier draft. I dedicate this work to Kathryn, Canon Chancellor of Portsmouth Cathedral.

Cambridge Elements ≡

The Philosophy of Ludwig Wittgenstein

David G. Stern

University of Iowa

David G. Stern is a Professor of Philosophy and a Collegiate Fellow in the College of Liberal Arts and Sciences at the University of Iowa. His research interests include history of analytic philosophy, philosophy of language, philosophy of mind, and philosophy of science. He is the author of *Wittgenstein's Philosophical Investigations: An Introduction* (Cambridge University Press, 2004) and *Wittgenstein on Mind and Language* (Oxford University Press, 1995), as well as more than 50 journal articles and book chapters. He is the editor of *Wittgenstein in the 1930s: Between the 'Tractatus' and the 'Investigations'* (Cambridge University Press, 2018) and is also a co-editor of the *Cambridge Companion to Wittgenstein* (Cambridge University Press, 2nd edition, 2018), *Wittgenstein: Lectures, Cambridge 1930–1933, from the Notes of G. E. Moore* (Cambridge University Press, 2016) and *Wittgenstein Reads Weininger* (Cambridge University Press, 2004).

About the Series

This series provides concise and structured introductions to all the central topics in the philosophy of Ludwig Wittgenstein. The Elements are written by distinguished senior scholars and bright junior scholars with relevant expertise, producing balanced and comprehensive coverage of the full range of Wittgenstein's thought.

Cambridge Elements ≡

The Philosophy of Ludwig Wittgenstein

Elements in the Series

A full series listing is available at: www.cambridge.org/EPLW

Printed in the United States
by Baker & Taylor Publisher Services